Songs for the Waiting

Songs for the Waiting

*Devotions Inspired by the
Hymns of Advent*

MAGREY R. DEVEGA

WESTMINSTER
JOHN KNOX PRESS
LOUISVILLE · KENTUCKY

© 2016 Magrey R. deVega

First edition
Published by Westminster John Knox Press
Louisville, Kentucky

16 17 18 19 20 21 22 23 24 25—10 9 8 7 6 5 4 3 2 1

Scripture quotations are from the Common English Bible, © 2011 Common English Bible, and are used by permission. Scripture quotations marked KJV are taken from the King James or Authorized Version of the Bible. Scripture quotations marked NRSV are taken from the New Revised Standard Version of the Bible, copyright 1989, Division of Christian Education of the National Council of the Churches of Christ in the United States of America. Used by permission. All rights reserved.

Excerpt from "O Come, O Come, Emmanuel" translation of verse 4 by Laurence Hull Stookey/Traditional © 1989 The United Methodist Publishing House (admin. by Music Services, Inc.) ASCAP. All rights reserved. Used by permission. Excerpt from "Prepare the Way of the Lord," by Taizé, © 1984 Les Presses de Taizé, France. GIA Publications, Inc., exclusive North American agent. All rights reserved. Used by permission. Excerpts from "I Want to Walk as a Child of the Light," by Kathleen Thomerson, © 1970, 1975 Celebration. All rights reserved. Used by permission. Excerpts from "People Look East," by Eleanor Farjeon, © 1960 David Higham Associates, Ltd. All rights reserved. Used by permission. Excerpts from "*Toda La Tierra*" (82861) © 1972, 1993 Centre De Pastoral Liturgica. Administered by OCP, 5536 NE Hassalo, Portland, OR 97213. All rights reserved. Used with permission. Excerpts from "To a Maid Engaged to Joseph," words: Gracia Grindal, © 1984 Hope Publishing Company, Carol Stream, IL 60188. All rights reserved. Used by permission. Reprinted under license #78081.

Book design by Drew Stevens
Cover design by Mary Ann Smith

Library of Congress Cataloging-in-Publication Data

Names: DeVega, Magrey R., author.
Title: Songs for the waiting : devotions inspired by the hymns of Advent / Magrey R. deVega.
Description: Louisville, KY : Westminster John Knox Press, 2016.
Identifiers: LCCN 2016006688 (print) | LCCN 2016014530 (ebook) | ISBN 9780664262525 (alk. paper) | ISBN 9781611646924 (e-book)
Subjects: LCSH: Advent hymns—History and criticism. | Advent—Biblical teaching.
Classification: LCC ML3186 .D35 2016 (print) | LCC ML3186 (ebook) | DDC 264/.23—dc23
LC record available at http://lccn.loc.gov/2016006688

Most Westminster John Knox Press books are available at special quantity discounts when purchased in bulk by corporations, organizations, and special-interest groups. For more information, please e-mail SpecialSales@wjkbooks.com.

For the people of
St. Paul's UMC in Cherokee, Iowa,
and Hyde Park UMC in Tampa, Florida

For Dad, Mom, Genniser, Mykel, Amanda, and Sara

And especially for Grace and Madelyn

Contents

Introduction

An ordinary trip to a department store turned into an intriguing moment of curiosity for my younger daughter Madelyn. We came across a display of record turntables.

"Wow! What is that?" Her eyes got bug-eyed with wonder.

You may remember these musical mainstays of the 1970s, back in the days when recording artists and music producers distributed the latest albums on vinyl records, complete with liner notes, album artwork, and B-side songs. I grew up listening to my parents' albums on our giant turntable, which doubled most of the time as a side table in our living room. (Some of these weren't just musical devices; they were giant pieces of furniture!) They are apparently making a comeback, as modern electronics companies have restarted the production and marketing of these essential parts of the Generation X / Baby Boomer childhood.

I offered my twelve-year old that little lesson on mid-twentieth-century pop culture, and in reply she said, "Ooooh. I want one!"

It's rare that a father is ever made to feel cool by his pre-teen daughter, so she was pushing all the right buttons.

With her thirteenth birthday just a month away, I purchased a brand-new turntable, along with a vinyl record by one of her favorite artists, and eagerly awaited the unveiling on her birthday. With great delight, she unwrapped the present, gleefully plugged it in, and watched studiously as I showed her how to make it work ("Turn the power on . . . raise the needle . . . set it on the edge of the record . . . and this switch adjusts your playback speed. . . .")

I'll have to admit that the sound quality of these new

machines far exceeds that which I remember back in the day. No scratchiness, no white noise, no whir of the turntable. When the opening track of the album started, the noise burst into the room, nearly matching the kind of sound generated by today's digital devices.

After losing myself in the music for a bit, I looked over at Madelyn. She was appreciative but pensive. After the first song was half over, I asked her, "So, what do you think?"

"It's good," she said, with a tone that suggested there was something more she wanted say. "So . . . how do you fast forward or skip to the next track?"

I bit my cheek to suppress the chuckle. "Well, there is no button to do that, so you have to pick up the needle, guess where the next track is, then manually move the needle over. And when the album is half-way finished, you have to flip the record over and start over."

"Oh."

It was a delightful learning moment. Not just for Madelyn, as she was introduced to the history (and to her, the *ancient* history!) of music playback machines. But it was a learning moment for me.

We live in a culture of perpetual fast-forwardness. We record our television shows to skip the commercials. We listen to albums à la carte. We forego handwriting letters in favor of 140-character tweets. We have steadily removed the need to wait in a culture where skipping ahead is the name of the game. In so doing, we have also diminished those moments of richness and fullness that come only with anticipation.

Perhaps there is no season of the year when that tendency is more evident than during Advent. Those four weeks begin the church's liturgical year with a call to patience and attentive preparation. As pregnancy precedes birth, so does Advent intentionally focus us on the ways to get ready for the arrival of Christ in and among us. We hear John the Baptist call us to prepare the way and make his paths straight. We listen to the prophets' calls to recalibrate our wayward paths back to holy and righteous living. We watch Zechariah, whose months of silent waiting prepare him for the birth of his son John. And we join with Mary in singing a song of obedience and praise.

These and many other stories of Advent are not meant to be glossed over, but that is what we often do when we skip too quickly to Bethlehem. We jump ahead to the birth, without making room for it.

And that is precisely what we often do with the songs and hymns of Advent.

Now, I am no liturgical purist when it comes to Christmas carols. I understand that people want to sing "Away in the Manger" and "O Little Town of Bethlehem" before Christmas Eve. Such songs evoke cherished memories of holidays gone by; and they nudge us toward a spirit of festive celebration, family connections, and joy. So I would never begrudge a congregation sprinkling in carols during Advent worship.

But when we do so at the expense of singing the Advent hymns, we are missing out on the rich message that only they can provide.

—When "O Come, O Come, Emmanuel" longs for Jesus to "ransom captive Israel," we acknowledge the ways that our souls are held captive and yearning for freedom.
—When "Come, Thou Long-Expected Jesus" envisions a savior who will "from our sins and fears release us," it offers a surgically precise diagnosis of our human condition.
—When "I Want to Walk as a Child of the Light" declares, "I want to see the brightness of God. / I want to look at Jesus," it is echoing the deepest longing and yearning of the human heart. A search for something greater than one's self, and a way out of the darkness of a wayward life.

This Advent, I invite you to refrain from fast-forwarding, and, instead, stay tuned in to the songs and stories of the season. Each of these twenty-eight daily readings, enough for the longest possible Advent, will be anchored by a line of an

Advent hymn, along with a text of Scripture. You may wish to sing that verse of the hymn, or listen to a recording, to prepare for reading the daily Scripture and to invite connections between the two. Taken together, they will prompt your own reflection on the ways that you might prepare for the fresh arrival of Jesus in your life.

Each devotional entry closes with a prayer and questions that you might answer in silence or in a journal; or you might choose to reflect on them with others in a small group. There is no greater enhancement to one's spiritual journey than to be accompanied by trusted sojourners along the way.

Whatever way you determine this book to be of help to you, resist the urge to skip on too quickly. Be intentional about the tending of your spirit and the cultivation of your soul. Let these songs and stories guide you to a deeper awareness of a God who wishes to draw you into a deeper connection with God and with all of life.

So let's fight the temptation to pick up the needle and skip ahead. The songs and stories of Advent await us. Let's take it a day at a time.

1

Forgive and Forget?

Read Psalm 137

O come, O come, Emmanuel,
and ransom captive Israel,
that mourns in lonely exile here
until the Son of God appear.
  —*"O Come, O Come, Emmanuel," verse 1*

Alongside Babylon's streams,
    there we sat down,
      crying because we remembered Zion.
We hung our lyres up
    in the trees there
      because that's where our captors asked us to sing;
      our tormentors requested songs of joy:
      "Sing us a song about Zion!" they said.
But how could we possibly sing
    the LORD's song on foreign soil?
                          —Psalm 137:1–4

Our journey begins with the best-known Advent hymn of
them all. Over and against the plastic good cheer of our com-
mercialized Christmas culture, the first verse of this hymn calls
us to acknowledge reality as we experience it: in mournfulness,
loneliness, captivity.

Often, those particular emotions run deepest in the context
of broken relationships with others. Perhaps, without even bat-
ting an eye, you can name instances in which you have been
wronged or where you have caused harm to someone else. In
these situations we often hear the old adage "forgive and forget."
It's a phrase intended to help us cope with these moments, and
you may have even offered that prescription to someone else.
But here's the problem: forgetting is impossible. To attempt to
do so would be to behave in contradiction to the way our God-
given minds are intended to work. Our capacity to remember
contributes to our survival, and it is simply not reasonable to

1

expect that we can switch our ability to remember on and off or to pick and choose what we will remember and what we will forget. The truth is, the more we *try* to forget about something that has happened to us, the more that memory becomes even *more* vivid and hard to forget.

A more possible—and perhaps more healing—course of action is to move those memories to the periphery, out of their position of governing influence in mind, heart, and spirit, to a place where the power they wield on us is lessened, and we can move on with confidence and joy, just as the chorus of "O Come, O Come, Emmanuel" suggests.

This concept of forgiveness is the connecting thread between the hymn and Psalm 137. In both, Israel is haunted by a longing for home, lured by the memories of what life was like before the hardship and suffering. Rather than inviting us to forget the past, these texts call us to embrace that longing and begin to hope for a brighter day ahead.

For you, Advent may be a time of pushing the difficult memories of your life to the periphery by longing for the arrival of new hope and promise. It involves daring to believe that God's light will come to you in real and unexpected ways, despite all the evidence to the contrary. And in those situations in which you find it difficult to believe in a God who comes near you as Emmanuel, then it is incumbent on you to surround yourself with people who can support you in your journey. People who can say to you, "Even though you have a hard time believing in God's faithfulness, I will believe it on your behalf until you are able to believe it for yourself."

That is why it is significant that Psalm 137 is written from the perspective of the first-person plural. "There *we* sat down . . . *our* captors asked *us* to sing . . ." To fully engage Advent this season, it is best to journey with companions. Look for people who can identify with your hurts, who will not judge you for the way you demonstrate your human struggles, and who can encourage you with truthfulness and love to change your attitude and your behavior.

Ultimately, Psalm 137 invites you into a simple exercise of naming and acknowledging the ways in which you experience exile in your life today. How are you longing for home? How do you find yourself in the midst of a "foreign land," surrounded by an environment that stifles your faith and fills you with doubt? Maybe you feel a temptation to succumb to the culture around you and give up on your faith, or at least water down your convictions to acquiesce to your surroundings. Maybe you can really identify with that first verse, and you simply feel like shedding a tear next to your figurative waters of Babylon.

As you name and acknowledge your own exile experience today, resist the temptation to escape it by seeking temporary pleasures or by trying to forget about them. Instead, lift up your exile experience in prayer, perhaps in a creative way. You might follow the lead of the psalm itself and sing "O Come, O Come, Emmanuel"—a song that captures that sense of longing for home—and offer that word and melody as an offering to God. You might simply choose to write about exile as a living record of how God is moving into and within your life, even in a foreign land.

The Diary of Anne Frank was just such a record of exile, a young girl describing her family's life in hiding during World War II. Anne did not use her journal as a way of ignoring her exile or forgetting about her pain. Instead, she used it as a way to both name her suffering and embrace hope. She exhibited a remarkable resilience in the way she anticipated life, especially in this entry:

> I want to be useful or bring enjoyment to all people, even those I've never met. I want to go on living even after my death! And that's why I'm so grateful to God for having given me this gift, which I can use to develop myself and to express all that's inside me![1]

This is the call of Advent: to surrender ourselves fully to a God who will come to set us free, to use our gifts for the benefit of others, and even to utilize our capacity to remember. For it is in remembrance of the past that we can claim healing for our future.

Reflection

In what ways are you experiencing captivity and exile in your life right now? What do you need to surrender to God in order to heal from the wounds of your past?

Prayer

Gracious God, thank you for your constant readiness to forgive and for the steadfastness of your grace. Teach me to forgive others, and myself, and to move into the abundant life you desire for all your people. Amen.

2

Wisdom Personified

Read Proverbs 3:13–20

O come, Thou Wisdom from on high,
and order all things, far and nigh;
to us the path of knowledge show
and cause us in her ways to go.
—*"O Come, O Come, Emmanuel," verse 2*

Happy are those who find wisdom
  and those who gain understanding.
Her profit is better than silver,
  and her gain better than gold.
Her value exceeds pearls;
  all you desire can't compare with her.
  —*Proverbs 3:13–15*

In Joseph Campbell's classic work *The Hero with a Thousand Faces*, the noted scholar on mythology and comparative religion described the Hero's Journey, a common theme in many of the most popular stories in Western civilization. The kinds of heroes involved in these stories vary, as do the context of their journeys, but they each contain a critical moment: the hero, having responded to a call to adventure, crosses the threshold from the known world into the world of the unknown.

In the midst of this season of ambiguity, the most formative experiences for the hero take place. But in Campbell's model, the hero is never alone. Soon after crossing that threshold, he or she is greeted by a helper, a sage, who guides the hero into the unknown and accompanies him or her through significant—and often painful—moments of transformation. Primarily, the helper provides to the hero wisdom born out of the experience of the past.

Movie fans can readily identify examples of how wisdom is personified in an actual person. Think about Yoda, who guides Luke in *Star Wars: The Empire Strikes Back*, Albus Dumbledore in the Harry Potter series, or Gandalf the wizard in The Lord of the Rings. The personification of wisdom in a particular character has permeated some of our favorite and most classic cinematic experiences. But whereas Yoda, Dumbledore, and Gandalf are all male (inasmuch as we are able to determine Yoda's gender), Proverbs renders Wisdom as female. In fact, the Hebrew word for *wisdom*, *hokmah*, is a feminine word. So, when Proverbs describes this woman, it is more accurately describing wisdom itself.

We read that she is more precious than riches (vv. 14–15). She offers longevity and honor (v. 16). And her paths are pleasant and peaceful (v. 17). Beyond this passage, Wisdom is regarded throughout Proverbs with great honor, as a source of life, hope, and transformation. And one of the key lessons of this book is clear: if you want true life—beyond the chaos, ambiguity, and confusion of the unknown—turn to Wisdom.

The composer of "O Come, O Come Emmanuel" reinforces this theme in the second verse. Anticipating the arrival of Jesus, this hymn considers the Messiah to be "Wisdom from on high, and orders all things, far and nigh." In essence, this hymn offers a parallel to the Hero's Journey of Joseph Campbell, in which all Advent pilgrims are on an adventure into and through the unknown.

Consider, then, how your life right now is like Luke Skywalker, or Harry Potter, or Frodo Baggins, or any of a number of famous heroes and heroines who have had to venture into the ambiguity of life. Perhaps your current situation is fraught with so much difficulty that you cannot perceive a way through it. Maybe your feet are swollen and bruised, the sweat beading on your furrowed brow, your eyes squinting through impenetrable darkness.

Both Proverbs and this hymn offer the same prescription:

seek Wisdom. Look for guidance to help you along your path. And don't look for it within yourself, because you will likely not find it in ample supply. Instead, look for it personified. Seek it in the life of another person, who can journey with you along your dark path.

When I think of such a person in my life, I give thanks to God for my Aunt Allan. She is my father's oldest sister and has been a spiritual rock for my whole extended family for as long as I can remember. She lost her husband in the military shortly after she gave birth to their two children, leaving her a single mother who would never remarry. Even as a youngster, I marveled at her ability to be so strong and independent, able to manage the concerns of parenthood along with all the difficulties of other family members.

How was she able to make it?

Prayer.

During a rather difficult stretch of time in my own life, Aunt Allan became my go-to person for wisdom personified. And though she is now in the twilight of her life, she maintains that rugged dependence on prayer that sustained her in the darkest days of her younger life. Whenever I call her for support and guidance, she is always ready for me. She is quick to offer me whatever Bible verse she had been pondering for my situation, and she inevitably reminds me of her devoted daily prayers for me.

I've always thought of her as my spiritual rock. But Proverbs and the second verse of this hymn would want me to consider her as a source of wisdom, because she draws me closer to Jesus.

No matter where you are in your dark times this Advent season, remember that you do not need to be alone. Seek out the wise counsel of a trusted companion, whether that person is a family member, friend, clergy person, therapist, or neighbor. You will find that having this person with you is indeed more precious than riches, a source of longevity, and a provider of peaceful pathways.

Reflection

Who embodies wisdom for you? How have you counted on these people for counsel, guidance, and encouragement in your life? In what ways might you serve as the embodiment of wisdom for someone else that you know?

Prayer

God of wisdom and strength, thank you for the ways that you have guided me along dark and lonely paths. Thank you for those who have served as light posts along my journey. And empower me to be the same for others. Amen.

3

Making Idols

Read Exodus 32:1–14

O come, O come, thou Lord of might,
who to thy tribes on Sinai's height
in ancient times didst give the law
in cloud and majesty and awe.
—*"O Come, O Come, Emmanuel," verse 3*

So all the people took out the gold rings from their ears and
brought them to Aaron. He collected them and tied them
up in a cloth. Then he made a metal image of a bull calf,
and the people declared, "These are your gods, Israel, who
brought you up out of the land of Egypt!"
—*Exodus 32:3–4*

Having negotiated the traumatic condition of exile, identified
our state of captivity, and named our need for Wisdom as a gift
from on high, the composer of "O Come, O Come Emmanuel" now turns our attention to the dry, dusty terrain of the
Sinai wilderness.

Here we locate one of the Bible's greatest narratives: the
liberation of the Israelites from Egyptian slavery. And among
the many tales of the Israelites in Sinai, one story summarizes
the sinfulness of the human condition.

The scene unfolds with the Israelites, having been led to
freedom from Pharaoh and Egypt and now wandering around
in the untamed desert. They are tired, confused, hungry, and
desperate. And worst of all, they feel abandoned: Abandoned
by Moses, because Moses has gone to the top of Mount Sinai
and hasn't been seen for days; abandoned by God, because
God has not told them to move for a very long time. So they
are stuck at the base of the mountain, and they feel alone.

We know, of course, that Moses and God have not abandoned the Israelites. They are having high-level conversations
about the Ten Commandments, but the rest of the people

don't know that. All they know is that Moses left, and he hasn't come back. Frankly, they don't know whether he is *ever* coming back.

So you know what they do next: They pool their gold together, and they build a statue that looks like a cow. And they set up a new congregation, the First United Heifer Church of Sinai.

We call it a golden calf, but the deeper problem here is not what the idol is made of or looks like, but what the idol symbolizes, and what it says about what they believe about God. They choose to believe in a god who is available and immediate and manufactured, rather than the real God who requires their patience and whom they experience as mysterious and beyond comprehension. They choose to believe in a god they can touch rather than a God they have to wait for. The essence of the golden calf is that they choose to believe in a god that they create rather than in the God who created them.

That is the one thing that all idols have in common. An idol for you is anything you create by your own power that puts God on your terms, that defines God in a way that is comfortable for you.

The Israelites suffered not only from spiritual laziness but also from spiritual amnesia. Because first and foremost, they forgot who God was.

They forgot that they didn't create themselves. None of us do.

They forgot they didn't save themselves. None of us can.

They forgot that they cannot provide for themselves. None of us will.

Only God can create, and save, and provide. And turning to idolatry is a symptom of our forgetfulness.

Advent challenges us to defy our expectations about God and the way God works. We might want God to come to us on our terms, at our own pace, but instead, God comes to us as a vulnerable baby, born in a small town, lying in a manger of hay.

This child, this Jesus, becomes the advocate that we need, whether we realize we needed one or not. An advocate like the one the Israelites had in Moses. When Moses saw how angry God was, he stepped up and pleaded on their behalf. "Remember, God, these are your people. You saved them. You called them. You will stick with them."

And Jesus, likewise, stepped into the gap and forged the possibility of a new relationship between a loving creator God and a people—like us—who would rather choose a different god. And in the end, "Then the LORD changed his mind about the terrible things he said he would do to his people" (Exod. 32:14).

Reflection

What idols have you created, even inadvertently, that make you forget the nature and work of God in your life? What steps can you take to remove those idols and offer God your full surrender?

Prayer

God of Abraham and Sarah, Isaac and Rebekah, and Jacob and Rachel, thank you for guiding your people through the wilderness and for guiding me through the struggles of life. Forgive me for the ways that I have forgotten who you are and what you wish to do in and through me. Amen.

4

More Than Meets the Eye

Read Samuel 16:1–13

O Come, thou Root of Jesse's tree,
an ensign of thy people be;
before thee rulers silent fall;
all peoples on thy mercy call.
—"O Come, O Come, Emmanuel," verse 4*

But the LORD said to Samuel, "Have no regard for his
appearance or stature, because I haven't selected him. God
doesn't look at things like humans do. Humans see only
what is visible to the eyes, but the LORD sees into the heart."
—1 Samuel 16:7

The fourth verse of "O Come, O Come, Emmanuel" offers a
quick trip up the ancestral family tree of Jesus. It is a rich and
varied genealogy, including names both notable and unfamil-
iar. But by far the greatest name among all of Jesus' ancestors is
David, offshoot of Jesse, the shepherd boy who would be king.

You would never know such greatness would come from
such an unassuming source.

And maybe that's the point.

A long time ago there lived a young boy. He grew up in
Denmark and, in his adolescent years, grew taller than the
other boys. He was sort of gawky and awkward, with a hawk-
ish nose and big feet. He wasn't into sports, but preferred the
arts, singing, writing, and performing in the theatre—all the
ingredients for becoming the target of cruel jabs and teasing by
the other kids. Being a teenager is tough enough, and it's even
worse when you stick out from the others.

The boy loved to write stories. We can imagine that he
wrote these stories to both escape and to capture the reality
of his private pain. But all the while, he knew a secret. This

young, awkward, brutally teased boy was no ordinary young man; he had royal blood. He was the illegitimate son of Christian Frederik, the Crown Prince of Denmark (later King Christian VIII of Denmark). And given his royal lineage, he wrote a story.

This story was about a little duckling who was uglier than his little duckling siblings. He was teased and taunted for being so different, so tall, and so awkward. And then one day, the duckling grew and grew into something else. A swan, it turns out; the most beautiful, regal, and royal looking of all of them.

Yes, you guessed it: this young man, born in Denmark in the nineteenth century, a mercilessly teased child who was royalty in the making, was Hans Christian Andersen, author of "The Ugly Duckling."

The Israelites' desire for a king produced Saul, whose outward appearance was everything they could want: strong and mighty, charismatic and captivating. But then they learned the hard way that it's not what's on the outside that counts. Because what you are on the inside will eventually come out. So God decided it was time to look for a new king, time to break the cycle of appearance addiction, the disease that rendered the Israelites unable to see what was truly on the inside.

God led Samuel to Bethlehem, to the house of Jesse, a good man with some great boys. One by one, he paraded them before the prophet. And one by one, they got turned down.

So Jesse said, "Well, there's one more. He's just a scrawny kid, sort of one we forget about. He sings well, has passion for the theater, is a writer; he's an ugly duckling, if you will, not in appearance but in the way he's treated by the others. He's just out with the sheep.

And the rest, as they say, is history. Like Hans Christian Andersen, this ugly duckling named David founded a royal lineage, although you'd never know by looking at his family tree.

David's great-grandmother was Ruth, an immigrant Moabite woman. His grandfather was Boaz, whose ancestors included a Canaanite woman who was almost executed for adultery and a Canaanite prostitute from Jericho named Rahab. Yet this shepherd boy became king, and he would become the ancestor of another ugly duckling. From Jesse's tree, a young boy would be born amid the scandal of two unmarried parents, one of them just a young girl. He would be born in a stable, among the animals, under the stars.

And today we call him king.

This story reminds us that God's grace is about more than meets the eye. It calls us to never settle for the easy outward appearance. Never take the easy shortcuts to power, prestige, and status by striving for mere good looks. Never take the cheaper and easier paths to peace and reconciliation and wholeness through violence or revenge. For God's grace is found in the unlikely places, like Emmanuel who grew from Jesse's questionable family tree to become one before whom "rulers silent fall" and people "on [his] mercy call."

It is a reminder to each of us that deep down inside even the ugliest persons among us is a child of God, waiting to be seen the way God sees him or her. Even the one who has hurt you or caused you heartache and resentment, God is at work in that person's life, whether you see it or not.

And God is at work in you as well. When you look in the mirror, maybe you see yourself the way your ducky siblings see you: awkward and gawky, weak and ungifted. Not worth much at all, they say. But you can believe this. You've been created in God's image, anointed for a purpose that you, and only you, can fulfill. God sees something in you, something you may not even see in yourself. And God is calling your name.

Reflection

How do the stories of the ugly duckling, the selection of David as king, and Jesus' own questionable heritage address any issues you have with low self-esteem or poor self-image?

Prayer

Gracious God, thank you for making me and all people in your image. Teach me to see myself through the lens of your grace and to see everyone I meet as your very own children. Amen.

5

Prepare the Way

Read Luke 3:2–6

Prepare the way of the Lord.
Prepare the way of the Lord,
and all people will see the salvation of our God.
—*"Prepare the Way of the Lord"*

This is just as it was written in the scroll of the words of
Isaiah the prophet,

A voice crying out in the wilderness:
"Prepare the way for the Lord;
make his paths straight."

—*Luke 3:4*

You would be hard pressed to find a Hallmark greeting card
with a picture of John the Baptist on the front.

Drive around your town at night, and it's likely you will not
find a house, decorated for Christmas, with a giant inflatable
man wearing camel skin.

And the next time someone at Target wishes you "Happy
Holidays," or a neighbor says to you, "Merry Christmas," I
doubt you would respond with a cheerful, "Repent, for the
kingdom of God is at hand!"

I'm not sure how he does it, but John the Baptist always
finds a way to weave himself into the discussion every Advent.
We may not like it; we may prefer placid scenes of shepherds on a starry night or angelic visits to Mary and Joseph.
Nonetheless, Advent wouldn't be Advent—and preparing for
Christmas just wouldn't be the same—without this wild man
from the wilderness.

He comes to us representing a tradition. His words and
actions are fully in line with the prophets of old, who spoke
controversial and uncomfortable words while performing
memorable, attention-grabbing actions. He eats locusts and
honey; he wears camel skin and leather. He emerges from the
wilderness and performs an odd ritual of dunking people into

the water. Whether we find him in Matthew, Mark, Luke, or John, his purpose is the same: to grab our attention and tell us to get ready.

His message rings out echoes of the prophet Isaiah: "Prepare the way of the Lord. Make his paths straight." In other words, your current trajectory is wayward, and the path you are currently traveling is crooked. You are headed toward a destination that will miss the mark of God's revelation in Jesus, and there is much work for you to do in order to be ready for Jesus' arrival.

That message is captured beautifully in the hauntingly repetitive melody by Jacques Berthier and the Taizé community. As you sing these words of John the Baptist, you can almost feel their recalibrating work sinking into your soul, to flush out the competing noises of your life and silence all other voices but those of God.

In fact, there may be no better way to ensure the preparedness of your soul in the busyness and hectic nature of life than to find more stillness and more silence.

Noted author and speaker Rob Bell has told a story about a man named Bernie Krause. Bernie Krause is a noted "soundscape artist." That is, he produces albums of sounds found in nature. Bernie reports that in 1968, in order to get one hour of natural sound—no cars, planes, or machines of any kind—it took about fifteen hours of recording time. Today, to get that same hour of natural sound, it requires over two thousand hours of recording time![1]

We are bombarded by the sounds of a noisy world, and it is becoming increasingly difficult to escape it. But this is nothing compared to the noise within us. How long would it take to record an hour of mental and emotional quiet in your mind and soul? Probably even longer than two thousand hours! We hear the constant drone of deadlines. We sense the thunderous booms of anxieties and fears, and the heavy pulsing of pressures, agendas, and to-do lists.

And over and against all this noise, a voice cries out from the wilderness, telling us to prepare for the coming of the Lord into our midst. We are called to make the ways straight, and to fill the valleys, and to smooth the rough places. And to that, we might add, we are called to silence the noise around us in order to hear the voice of God.

A story is told about the origins of a well-known African proverb:

> Some adventurers got together and planned an African safari. They saved their money, bought tickets, mapped out their safari, and hired an African guide and porters. They arose early in the morning to begin their trek deep into the jungle. They pressed hard the first day.
>
> When the sun went down, they pitched their tents and set up camp for the night. Early the next morning, the adventurers were ready to go again, eager with anticipation to get farther into the jungle and see more wild animals. They noticed that the porters, though, would not move. In frustration, one of the adventurers went and asked the guide, "What's the problem?"
>
> The guide informed him that they had gone too fast the first day, and that they were now waiting for their souls to catch up with their bodies.

Maybe this Advent, you need to wait for your soul to catch up.

Maybe the way for you to prepare the way for the Lord is to slow down, and stop, and pay attention to the sirens in your rearview mirror.

Reflection Questions

What is preventing you from "preparing the way of the Lord" by inviting more silence and stillness into your life this Advent? What will it take for your "soul to catch up"?

Prayer

Gracious God, thank you for sending us this alarming, attention-getting word from John the Baptist. Teach me how to slow down, listen up, and silence all voices but yours. Amen.

6

Desensitized to Hope

Read 1 Thessalonians 5:1–11

I want to walk as a child of the light.
I want to follow Jesus.
God set the stars to give light to the world.
The star of my life is Jesus.
—*"I Want to Walk as a Child of the Light,"* verse 1

All of you are children of light and children of the day. We
don't belong to night or darkness.
—*1 Thessalonians 5:5*

The author of the hymn writes from the perspective of the first
person and makes an impassioned appeal: "I want to walk as a
child of the light; I want to follow Jesus." The author does not
say, "I have it all figured out." Or, "I am already in the light."

Instead, this is a voice from one who admits to being in the
dark and yearns for new light. It offers encouragement to those
who find themselves lost and in need of the light of God. All
that is needed is desire and openness to that light.

There is a powerful scene toward the end of *The Last Battle*, the conclusion of C. S. Lewis' famous Chronicles of Narnia series. The children arrive at the dwelling of the Narnian
dwarves, a collection of sour, miserable, scowling creatures who
are the antagonists of the story. They find the dwarves huddled
together, in a circle, facing inward, refusing to acknowledge
the light and beauty around them, and focusing only on their
own despondency.

The children are perplexed by the dwarves' self-imposed
darkness. "But it isn't dark, you poor stupid Dwarfs," says
Lucy. "Can't you see? Look up! Look round! Can't you see the
sky and the trees and the flowers? Can't you see *me*?"[1]

But the children's attempts to convince the dwarves of the

light don't work. Despite all rational reasoning and evidence of the beauty around them, the dwarves continue to live in a sad, artificial exile, in pure denial of any reality but the one they have created and chosen.

Eventually, the lion Aslan shows up—the great hero and Christ-figure of the Narnia series. There is a sudden flash of lightning, a trembling of the earth, and a sweetness in the air. Lucy asks Aslan to "do something for these poor Dwarfs," and he instantly provides a feast of scrumptious foods for them. The Dwarfs hungrily take it all in, but just as their sense of sight was blind to the beauty around them, their taste buds are virtually inoperative, rendering all the delicious foods undesirable.

Aslan concludes with this sad assessment: "They will not let us help them. They have chosen cunning instead of belief. Their prison is only in their own minds, yet they are in that prison; and so afraid of being taken in that they cannot be taken out."[2]

This scene provides a potent descriptor of the human condition and further reason why the Advent journey is so necessary. Like the dwarves, the darkness in our lives has so desensitized our ability to see the beauty of God's grace and forgiveness that we focus only on grief, despair, hopelessness, and tragedy. Advent calls us to acknowledge those realities but not to dwell on them and not to assign them more power than they actually have. Instead, we are called to reorient our attentiveness toward the possibility of the light that is to come into our midst.

That is the theme of both Paul's letter to the Thessalonians, and the first verse of "I Want to Walk as a Child of the Light." Even the opening words "I want to . . ." conjure up and capture the kind of longing inherent in Advent: the hope that something is out there, beyond our capacity to create it, that will lift us out of an existence in which we are desensitized to hope.

It should be no surprise that both the hymn and the epistle base those convictions on the image of light, because that is a recurring symbol throughout the biblical narrative: God's first creation in the beginning of the world, the pillar of fire that lit up the darkened sky to lead the Hebrews out of slavery, the light the prophets promised would come, the light that blinded Saul and turned his life around.

Advent is filled with lights: the lights of our Christmas trees, our Advent wreath candles, and our house decorations. Each time you see a Christmas light, give thanks to God for the arrival of this Jesus, who comes as a light into the midst of our darkness and draws us out of our desensitized, hopeless existence, into the reality of God's grace and forgiveness.

And then, just as the hymn and the epistle encourage us, commit to becoming a "child of the light," in which you become the very conduit through which God's light can be shared with others.

Reflection

The opening words of today's hymn are, "I want to. . . ." Do you identify with that kind of longing for connection with God? Why or why not?

Prayer

God of light and love, thank you for offering the world the gift of light in Jesus. Teach me to accept that gift and refuse to live in darkness. And help me be a bearer of that same light for others. Amen.

7

Following the Way

Read John 14:1–7

I want to see the brightness of God.
I want to look at Jesus.
Clear Sun of righteousness, shine on my path,
and show me the way to the Father.
—*"I Want to Walk as a Child of the Light," verse 2*

Jesus answered, "I am the way, the truth, and the life. No
one comes to the Father except through me. If you have
really known me, you will also know the Father. From now
on you know him and have seen him."

—*John 14:6–7*

Having expressed a desire to see the light of Jesus and to follow him, the Advent hymn then makes a subtle shift to another predominant metaphor for Christ in the Gospels. "Shine on my path and show me the way to the Father."

When we think of the image of "the way" in relation to Jesus, we can make an immediate connection to the words of Jesus in John 14: "I am the way, the truth, and the life. No one comes to the Father but through me."

Perhaps no other passage in John's Gospel more clearly states his central premise about who Jesus Christ is and how we are to respond. On one level, we might claim to know what Jesus is saying here. There is a right way to go, and there is a wrong way. There is a right way to go to get to the Father, and that way is through Jesus. Regardless of the direction that others choose to travel, we must go the way of Jesus if we are to find real life, a life in relationship with God.

But as significant as this text is for John's Gospel, it is not without its controversy. Many Christians throughout the history of the church have used it as a theological litmus test to gauge the true followers of Jesus from the imposters; or worse, to evaluate who is going to heaven and who is not.

In our world today, filled with many religious options and a veritable smorgasbord of religions and faiths, Christians have used this text as an exclusionary hammer, condemning, judging, and sentencing people to hell. But interpretation misses the original point of the passage. The first Christians were not Gentiles. They were Jews. They were people who grew up in the traditions of ancient Israel, with the Temple, the synagogue, the Torah, the festivals, and the feasts. As word about Jesus began to spread, these Jews had to make a choice. Follow this Jesus movement or stay true to Judaism?

These first followers of Jesus were not even called *Christians*. That title would come much later. Instead, they were called, "People of the Way" or "Followers of the Way." They were Jews who decided that this way of Jesus was the way to live.

Making that choice had consequences. It often led to banishment from the synagogue, or from one's hometown, or, worst of all, from one's own family. The followers of Jesus were condemned, despised, often at the cost of tearing apart families and neighborhoods. As a result, many of the first Christians were tempted, tempted to go back to their old way of believing and living. They were tempted to turn around, do a U-turn, and go with the traffic again, rather than against it; they were tempted to go another way, rather than the way of Jesus.

When John first wrote these words, they were intended to be more than a theological litmus test to determine who was going to heaven and who was not. They were certainly not meant to be tools for condescension as they are used today. Instead, these words were intended to serve as encouragement to those who were tempted to leave their convictions behind and forsake their beliefs in Jesus.

Here is another way to say it, for us modern-day followers of the Way: Don't give up. Don't leave behind your convictions about Jesus. It may be too easy, too comfortable, and too convenient to choose another way, particularly in a culture where it is the norm to do so. But don't go back. Stay true to the Way. Keep on going.

The path that Jesus shows us is the way of love.

Remember that these verses in John 14 follow an important teaching Jesus gave to the disciples in John 13. In the upper room, following the Last Supper, Jesus said this to them:

> "Little children, I'm with you for a little while longer. You will look for me—but, just as I told the Jewish leaders, I also tell you now—'Where I'm going, you can't come.'
>
> "I give you a new commandment: Love each other. Just as I have loved you, so you also must love each other." (John 13:33–34)

To follow the way of Jesus is to love, and it is a way that leads to a cross. It means putting to death all in our lives that leads to self-destruction and harm in our relationships with others. It means surrendering our will to a God who calls us to love those who are different from us, even if they have wronged us. It means taking a risk to love the unlovable, regardless of the cost.

And it means refusing to go back to the way we were before.

So, fellow followers of the Way, don't stop. Don't turn around, and don't go back. Follow the way of truth, and by all means, live a life of love.

Reflection

In what ways are you tempted to compromise your convictions about Jesus because of pressures from the culture around you? What challenges do you experience as you follow the way of Jesus?

Prayer

Lord Jesus, thank you for being the way, the truth, and the life. Help me to walk in that way, despite temptations from around me and within me to do otherwise. In all things, empower me to carry my cross and follow you. Amen.

8

Catching Fireflies

Read John 11:32–44

I'm looking for the coming of Christ.
I want to be with Jesus.
When we have run with patience the race,
we shall know the joy of Jesus.
— *"I Want to Walk as a Child of the Light," verse 3*

He asked, "Where have you laid him?"
They replied, "Lord, come and see."
Jesus began to cry. The Jews said, "See how much he loved him!"
— *John 11:34–36*

The third verse of "I Want to Walk as a Child of the Light" captures the sentiment of a person drawing close to the twilight of life. The phrase "when we have run with patience the race" suggests the end of a life well lived, seeking security in the love and grace of Jesus Christ.

We who still walk on the finite and imperfect side of a broken world, where bodies still break down and where death still pervades, find ourselves confronting the inevitable nature of our own mortality. It has to be this kind of moment that greeted Jesus when he finally decided to go to Bethany in today's Scripture storytelling.

You know how the story goes. Lazarus was dying, Mary and Martha made a pitch for Jesus to come to them, but Jesus chose to wait. Not out of callous indifference to the family—in fact, we find out he truly loved Mary, Martha, and Lazarus— but in order to make a point. It's a point that is hard for us to hear when we are captivated by grief. But this point makes all the difference in the world and all the difference to eternity.

When Jesus arrived, Mary and Martha were grieving. They were angry, quite understandably angry, perhaps at Jesus, but more at the unfairness of it all. And Jesus was there, to sit, to listen, to gather the stories, to identify with the struggles.

24

I have to say, of all the privileges that we as pastors observe in our profession, it is precisely this moment, sitting with the grieving, that is our most sacred privilege. The time I spend with a family to plan a funeral is one of the most important, most sacred occasions in my job. I am there to serve as a counselor, a resident theologian, and a pastoral wordsmith. Every critical component of my calling to ministry is represented in that hallowed hour. Most of all, I am there to elicit and gather stories that capture the family's fullest remembrance of their loved one.

This kind of storytelling and story gathering is critical in the grieving process. Families will share a story immediately as it comes to mind, hoping that in its uttering, it can be captured and preserved. Like catching fireflies on a summer night, they work quickly to capture the stories that might become the small, flickering lights they can cherish in the midst of their darkness.

And that is exactly the dynamic at play when the story of Jesus and Mary and Martha takes its surprising turn. The very first thing that Martha expresses to Jesus is understandable grief and anger. "Lord, if you had been here, my brother wouldn't have died." But in that same breath, in the same sentence, like a firefly at night, a new insight captures her mind. "Even now I know that whatever you ask God will give you. I know that he will rise in the resurrection on the last day."

You see, we Christian people believe that when we walk on this side of the grave, we do so in the shadow of eternity. Even as we "run with patience the race," we look toward the joy of being with Jesus. We claim that though we live in finite and mortal days, when bodies break down and death prevails, we live with the light of eternity in our hearts. And that means that the power of the resurrection and the promise of new life is not simply something that awaits us when we die but can inform our hope and even our behavior in the way we live today.

Eternity can shape our mortality. The future can inform our present. The promise of God's glory yet to be revealed can actually be experienced today in the way we live and love one another.

When we talk about "running the race" during Advent, we may think less of a long and faithful lifetime and more of the rat race that preparing for Christmas has become. We rush around to buy the presents and mail the cards and bake the cookies and make at least a hasty showing at the parties. But we know that's not what really matters in the end.

There is one common facet among all the stories I hear from families who have just lost a loved one. Loved ones aren't remembered for their possessions or their achievements, not their gadgets or their toys, or their properties or portfolios, not their successes or their trophies, or their distinctions or their diplomas. None of those things ever seems to matter when it comes to important family memories.

What does a family remember the most? They remember the relationships, the people, the people impacted by their loved one's talents and time, those who were privileged enough to be within that person's sphere of influence—each person who says, "I will never be the same because that person was in my life."

This Advent, let's focus on investing more in those relationships with people. Cherish the relationships you have with those around you. Forget the rat race and focus on the patient, faithful journey we take together that leads to Jesus.

Reflection

What are you investing your time and resources in right now that, in light of eternity, may not make a lot of difference in the end? With which people do you need to spend more time and effort in strengthening your relationships?

Prayer

God of time and space, thank you for walking with me, step-by-step, through the highs and lows of life. Help me to keep eternity in mind and to focus on things that will really matter in the lives of others. Amen.

9

Jesus' Inaugural Address

Read Luke 4:14–30

Hail to the Lord's Anointed, great David's greater Son!
Hail in the time appointed, his reign on earth begun!
He comes to break oppression, to set the captive free;
to take away transgression, and rule in equity.
—*"Hail to the Lord's Anointed," verse 1*

The Spirit of the Lord is upon me,
    because the Lord has anointed me.
He has sent me to preach good news to the poor,
    to proclaim release to the prisoners
    and recovery of sight to the blind,
    to liberate the oppressed,
    and to proclaim the year of the Lord's favor.
—*Luke 4:18–19*

"The only thing we have to fear is fear itself." (Franklin D. Roosevelt, 1933)

"I have nothing to offer but blood, toil, tears and sweat." (Winston Churchill, 1940)

"Ask not what your country can do for you, but ask what you can do for your country." (John F. Kennedy, 1961)

When *Time* magazine published its list of the greatest political speeches in history, it wasn't surprising to see Roosevelt's, Churchill's, and Kennedy's first addresses after taking office among them. Their words inspired people eager to hear their visions for the future and anxious to be lifted out of a current crisis. Every time a new president is elected, that person takes the same anticipated stage, with the same captivated attention.

Years ago, Wang Chien-Chuang, president of *The Journalist* magazine, wrote that there are a few key ingredients to every successful political speech:

1. You need a good speechwriter.
2. The speech must be delivered before the backdrop of some great national crisis.
3. It has to include a substantial declaration of policies.[1]

The opening verse of "Hail to the Lord's Anointed" brims with the kind of pomp, pageantry, and expectation often associated with a presidential inauguration, and in fact, it echoes the very words that Jesus spoke in his very first sermon. In some ways, we might even consider his first sermon, recorded for us in Luke 4, as his inaugural address. Not a political speech, Jesus' first sermon offered, nonetheless, his opening remarks to a people immersed in a politically charged time.

So, how does Jesus' speech rank, according to Wang Chien-Chuang's criteria?

1. First, you need a good speechwriter. For his speechwriter, Jesus selected one of the best. He chose the prophet Isaiah, the most significant name to the Jewish people in the previous six hundred years. The mere mention of his name would have conjured feelings of solemn reverence and obedience to God. Isaiah had spoken to the people in times of national crisis and comforted them with a vision of hope for the future. For imagery, poetry, substance, and style, Jesus could not have selected a better wordsmith.

2. Second, the speech should be delivered before the backdrop of some great national crisis. It was not the Great Depression, World War II, or the civil rights movement, but it was indeed a time of great turmoil. When Jesus stepped before the congregation in that synagogue, his was a world immersed in crisis. The Jewish people had become unwilling pawns in a global power game, ruled by the Babylonians, the Persians, the Seleucids, the Hasmoneans, the Greeks, and now, Rome. And worse than their political persecution, they were in spiritual crisis. Where was God in all of this? Where was the faithfulness of the God they believed in?

When Jesus began his public ministry, he did not come when it was most convenient and most comfortable. The world was at its most dangerous, and the situation was at its most precarious.

3. It has to include a substantial declaration of policies. Great speeches have not only style but also substance, not only a broadly stroked vision but also a summons to specifics. So what constituted Jesus' plan for action?

—The poor in the community will hear good news.
—Those who are held captive will be released.
—The blind will be able to see again.
—The oppressed will be set free.
—God's favor will be proclaimed to all the people.

And then, in the boldest moment in the entire speech, Jesus sat down and delivered his FDR/JFK line: "Today this Scripture has been fulfilled in your hearing."

Suddenly, Jesus' address transcended mere political rhetoric and future-oriented optimism. He dared to claim that the promise of tomorrow was fulfilled in the present. Whereas most figures can only make promises and hope to keep them, or share visions and hope to see them made real, Jesus boldly proclaimed that all these things had already happened! The reign of the Lord's Anointed had already begun.

Advent is a time of anticipation, in which we dare to expect that the arrival of Jesus will fulfill the dreams and hopes of a people longing for new life. And the way we will evaluate the fulfillment of that promise is in the tangible difference that Jesus will make through us, throughout the world. Will the poor hear good news? Will those held captive find release? Will those blinded by darkness rediscover their sight? And will every oppressed person everywhere claim freedom?

May these questions constitute your prayers and guide our actions as we await the coming of the Messiah. So that today, indeed, these promises might be fulfilled in our hearing.

Reflection Questions

Consider the policy declarations that Jesus makes in his first sermon. Which ones most resonate with your own personal situation or in your community? Where have you personally seen evidence of Christ fulfilling those promises?

Prayer

Loving God, we thank you for the compelling witness of your prophets, who foretold of your saving restoration of the world. Empower us to see evidence of your work around us and then to participate in that restoration with you. Amen.

10

Why Worry?

Read Luke 12:22–34

He comes with succor speedy to those who suffer wrong;
to help the poor and needy, and bid the weak be strong;
to give them songs for sighing, their darkness turn to light,
whose souls, condemned and dying, are precious in his sight.
—*"Hail to the Lord's Anointed," verse 2*

Don't chase after what you will eat and what you will drink.
Stop worrying. All the nations of the world long for these
things. Your Father knows that you need them. Instead,
desire his kingdom and these things will be given to you as
well.

—*Luke 12:29–31*

It is quite possible that the second verse of "Hail to the Lord's
Anointed" is the verse you need to hear today, at this point in
your Advent journey. Each word, each phrase, can be like a
salve for a weary soul and an apt descriptor for where you are
today:

> . . . those who suffer wrong
> . . . to help the poor and needy
> . . . bid the weak be strong
> . . . to give them songs for sighing
> . . . souls, condemned and dying

Couple these phrases with the words of Jesus to his disciples
in Luke 12, and we receive comfort for worn, strained lives.
For anyone burdened by the trials of everyday living, and for
every worried soul anxious about the future, these words provide the hope and promise that is at the heart of Advent.

The history of the church is filled with saints whose lives
serve as an example to us of the life of faith. And when it comes

to learning how to live with less worry and more hope, few saints offer a better a model for us than St. Francis de Sales.

Francis de Sales was a Frenchman born in 1567, and after studying both law and theology in Paris, he dedicated his life to the priesthood. It was a decision that surprised his parents, and the pastorate was not initially a natural fit for him. One historian characterized his preaching by saying, "When he preached, the listeners thought he was making fun of them." And people began to complain to the bishop that de Sales was too conceited and controlling. Throughout his efforts to build the kingdom in the ripe mission field of Protestant Geneva, Switzerland, he had doors slam in his face and people throw rocks at him. In the bitter winters, his feet froze so badly they bled as he tramped through the snow. He slept in haylofts if he could, but once he slept in a tree to avoid wolves. He tied himself to a branch to keep from falling out and was so frozen the next morning he had to be cut down.

After three years of evangelizing, he had not made one convert. But de Sales did not quit, and he did not worry. Because he could not get a face-to-face audience with people, he wrote his sermons down, reproduced them, and slid them underneath people's doors. To this day, he is known as the patron saint of writers, editors, and journalists because of his printed efforts.

Over time, his spiritual journey brought him to Christian mysticism, and he developed a passion for spiritual direction. People, clergy and lay alike, began to come to him to learn how to practice the devout life and to hear the voice of God. He is credited during this time period as opening the way of spiritual practice and holiness and devotion to common people, lay-people. When it was thought that spiritual piety was reserved only for the professionally religious, de Sales offered all people the way to practice this kind of holy life. Because he believed that it was possible for laypeople to be fully engaged spiritually while observing the demands of secular work, he spent much time guiding people through the barriers and obstacles of daily demands, deadlines, and stress.

You can name for yourself those things that you are worried

about at this moment. We all have a long list: personal concerns; family struggles; church issues; physical, economic, relational, emotional, mental, and spiritual battles.

In a pamphlet, *Wise and Loving Counsels*, de Sales offered words that can address the deepest part of our worry today:

> Do not look forward to the mishaps of this life with anxiety, but await them with perfect confidence so that when they do occur, God, to whom you belong, will deliver you from them. He has kept you up to the present; remain securely in the hand of his providence, and he will help you in all situations. When you cannot walk, he will carry you. Do not think about what will happen tomorrow, for the same eternal Father who takes care of you today will look out for you tomorrow and always. Either he will keep you from evil or he will give you invincible courage to endure it.
>
> Remain in peace; rid your imagination of whatever troubles you.
>
> Belong totally to God. Think of him and he will think of you. He has drawn you to himself so that you may be his; he will take care of you. Do not be afraid, for if little chicks feel perfectly safe when they are under their mother's wings, how secure should the children of God feel under his paternal protection! So be at peace, since you are one of these children; and let your weary, listless heart rest against the sacred, loving breast of this Savior who, by his providence is a father to his children, and by his gentle, tender love is a mother to them.[1]

These are powerful words from a person who exemplifies courage, toughness, and stamina in the midst of hardships. In whatever you are facing today, may you depend on the One who "comes with succor speedy."

Reflection

What brings you great worry right now during this Advent season? How might you begin to offer God the source and circumstance of your worry?

Prayer

God of Provision and Promise, I confess to you that I am too prone to worry. Grant me the strength to offer my concerns to you. And then give me both the wisdom and the strength to prevent those worries from resurfacing in my life. Amen.

11

Rains of Peace

Read Psalm 85

He shall come down like showers upon the fruitful earth;
love, joy, and hope, like flowers, spring in his path to birth.
Before him on the mountains, shall peace, the herald, go,
and righteousness, in fountains, from hill to valley flow.
— *"Hail to the Lord's Anointed," verse 3*

Faithful love and truth have met;
   righteousness and peace have kissed.
Truth springs up from the ground;
   righteousness gazes down from heaven.

—Psalm 85:10–11

The third verse of "Hail to the Lord's Anointed" reads a lot like an issue of *National Geographic*. It is earthy, picturesque, and organic, with images of rain showers and fruitful lands, blooming flowers and looming mountains, and flowing rivers coursing from hills to valleys.

Often, the Bible uses these kinds of topographical images to describe the state of the human soul. And like this verse of the hymn, Psalm 85 offers a description of life from a person seeking to find and understand God's peace within his or her life.

You, the God who can save us, restore us! Stop being angry with us! Will you be mad at us forever? Will you prolong your anger from one generation to the next? Won't you bring us back to life again (Psalm 85:4–6)?

The psalmist describes a soul that is parched and dry. The psalm speaks of spiritual drought, of a yearning for nourishment and revival. It describes a person who has exhausted all physical and mental resources to try and make it through life and is almost at the end of his or her rope.

It is believed by some scholars that Psalm 85 is actually a prayer for rain, not only for physical, environmental rain but, more important, for rain in a spiritual sense. All that the psalmist has left, after battling through life and jumping over one hurdle after another, is fatigue, fear, worry, and a simple prayer to God for the rain's blessings and peace to fall again in life.

What does God's peace look like? For the psalmist, it looks like rain, like "showers upon the fruitful earth," as librettist James Montgomery put it in today's hymn.

Do you hear it? Do you sense the connection between the falling of rain and the giving of God's peace? More important, is that what you are searching for today? Peaceful rain upon your parched and dry soul?

It is an interesting connection, peace and rain.

— Rain falls from the sky and nourishes the ground. God's peace falls from God's hand and quenches our thirsty souls.
— Rain collects in and fills our seas and rivers. God's peace collects in and fills our hearts with an abundance of comfort and joy.
— Rain washes the earth and removes from it refuse pollutants from the soil. God's peace washes over us and through us and makes us clean.
— Rain causes plants to blossom, trees to grow, and flowers to blossom. God's peace enables whatever within us that is dying and decaying to spring forth into new life.

Truth springs up from the ground; righteousness gazes down from heaven, the psalmist proclaims.

Do you need to pray for rain today?

Let us consider for a moment that this psalm is not about the psalmist but about us. We could have very easily penned these words for ourselves. We are in need of the rain of God's peace in our lives. The psalmist gives us good advice:

First, remember. Use your memories. Recall the things God has done for you before. The psalmist begins this song by recalling how God had saved the people before and how God has been faithful in delivering and saving people from tragedy.

Certainly God has granted you many blessings in your life. And the inability to remember them right now is not from lack of occurrence but from lack of remembrance.

What are the moments in your life when you can say with certainty, "God has come through for me. I may not have recognized it at the time, but God has pulled me through"?

The first three verses of Psalm 85 read like a résumé, like a scrapbook of God's saving acts:

> LORD, you've been kind to your land;
>> you've changed Jacob's circumstances for the better.
> You've forgiven your people's wrongdoing;
>> you've covered all their sins.
> You've stopped being furious;
>> you've turned away from your burning anger.

You can rest assured that the God who was faithful in your past will be faithful again. Claim that reality and find God's peace today.

The other encouragement is to listen. The psalmist says,

> Let me hear what the LORD God says,
>> because he speaks peace to his people and to his faithful
>> ones.
> Don't let them return to foolish ways. (v. 8)

God is speaking to you a word of comfort and peace at this very moment. You must not believe that God is absent from your life. Rather, God has never been closer. God is speaking to us peace and faithfulness. And we can hear those words, if only we would hush the drowning noise around us and hear the words of God.

Reflection

When have you experienced a prolonged period of drought, either literally (in relation to the weather) or spiritually (in relation to our doubts, disbeliefs, and concerns)? Can you hear the voice of God's peace in your life right now?

Prayer

God of Sunshine and Rain, you see your people struggling through periods of prolonged doubt and disbelief. Help me to learn to trust you in the midst of my own drought so that I can learn to antici-pate the rain of your love and grace. Amen.

12

Claiming the Future

Read Exodus 12:1–14

People, look east. The time is near of the crowning of the year.
Make your house fair as you are able; trim the hearth and set the table.
People, look east and sing today: Love, the Guest, is on the way.
                                        —*"People, Look East," verse 1*

This is how you should eat it. You should be dressed, with your
sandals on your feet and your walking stick in your hand. You
should eat the meal in a hurry. It is the Passover of the LORD.
                                        —*Exodus 12:11*

Back in 1904, a pious Christian woman named Margaret
Sangster, a Sunday school teacher and devotional writer, published what turned out to be a wildly popular etiquette book
for Christian ladies and gentlemen. She wanted to teach polite
Christians practical advice about how to behave in certain
social circumstances.

For example, she offers this advice on how to eat a meal:

> Do not annoy those sitting next to you by fidgeting in your
>   chair, drumming with your fingers on the table, laugh-
>   ing uproariously or playing with your bread.
> Do not chew your food with your mouth open, and when
>   you are eating do not make any of the noises associated
>   with vulgarity.
> As for alcoholic beverages, they are permissible only
>   when prescribed for medicinal purposes by a reputable
>   physician.
> When you are eating, keep your other hand quietly on your
>   lap, your mind composed and fastened pleasantly on
>   the conversation. Let all of your movements be easy and
>   deliberate. Hasty movements are the sign of a nervous
>   disorder.[1]

Now, from a distance, we might see Mrs. Sangster (God rest her soul) as quaintly irrelevant. At the very least, we might call these rules a little odd.

You want to know what else is odd? The rules for how God says the people of God were to come to the table.

In Exodus 12, the Israelites are told that when you come to the table, keep your belt on tight. Keep your sandals on and the staff in your hand, for you should eat in a hurry. Be ready, the Passover of the Lord, the deliverance of God, is about to happen, and you don't want to miss it.

Odd stuff? Perhaps. But what is even stranger than the instructions themselves is where they are placed in the story of Exodus.

Biblical scholars would say that these verses are the prescription for how to observe the Passover ritual. They are instructions for worship, guidelines for what to do when the community comes together when it observes the Passover. But here's the odd part: These instructions are given *before* the Passover actually happens.

That's not the way it works. You have the event, and *then* you have the remembrance. You have the signing of the Declaration of Independence, and *then* you declare the July 4 holiday. You have the birth of George Washington, and *then* you have President's Day. You have the life of the Rev. Dr. Martin Luther King Jr., and *then* you have MLK Day. You have the event, and *then* you have. . . .

But not here.

Instead, here in Exodus, the Israelites are given specific instructions on how to behave in anticipation of something that God guarantees in the future. And God is so sure that it will happen that you best be ready for it; don't let it catch you off guard. When you gather as a community, cinch your belt tight. Keep a staff in your hand and your sandals on. Be ready.

Only in Christian community do we have the opportunity to practice rituals that anticipate the future. It was the case for the Israelites at Passover, and it is the case here for us. So much of what we do every Sunday is in remembrance and celebration of something that has not yet even happened. When we recite a creed together, we claim these words as sacred in holy trust, and we lean into them in the belief that their truths will be fully realized in our lives. When we share in the reading of Scripture, we allow its messages to sink deep into our souls, preparing for its time-released power to be discharged. When we pray with one another, we do so in faith, knowing that our very act of prayer is a reach into the unknown and its consequences will be revealed somehow in the future. Faith is about celebrating things that will happen down the road.

So whenever we get together, it is not just to remember something that has already happened but to anticipate the dawn of something new, exciting, and transformative.

That, in essence, is the spirit of Advent.

Eleanor Farjeon's Advent hymn "People, Look East" begins with precisely that call to preparation. She uses the imagery of preparing a house for the arrival of a guest, which is a wonderful metaphor for the season. Just as we trim our trees, set our decorations, and hang lights to create a festive atmosphere, Advent calls us to make similar preparations within our spirits and with fellow Christians to get ready for what God will do in and among us.

So, we must be ready. Keep our belts on tight and put the sandals on our feet. Put the staff in our hands and eat hurriedly. The Lord is about to do something great!

Reflection Questions

Consider the last time you planned or attended a bridal or baby shower. Think about how those celebrations anticipate future events. How does worship do the same? How is Advent also a celebration of something that has not yet happened?

Prayer

Eternal God, thank you for filling my life with such hope so that I am able to live out my faith today in anticipation of your future yet to be revealed. Teach me to be faithful to you in every present moment. Amen.

13

What Comes Down Will Rise Up

Read John 12:24–26

Furrows, be glad. Though earth is bare,
   one more seed is planted there.
Give up your strength the seed to nourish,
   that in course the flower may flourish.
People, look east and sing today: Love, the Rose, is on the way.
            —*"People, Look East," verse 2*

I assure you that unless a grain of wheat falls into the earth and
dies, it can only be a single seed. But if it dies, it bears much
fruit.

             —*John 12:24*

The second verse of "People, Look East" centers on one of the
Gospel's most common symbols: a seed. It is a single seed that
is planted in the ground with the hope that, against all odds, it
will grow. "The earth is bare," the hymn says, and it requires a
heavy investment of strength in order for the seed to be nour-
ished and for the flower to flourish.

The verse echoes many parables of the kingdom of God, in
which a sower sows seeds that fall on four kinds of soil or when
the kingdom is compared to the mustard seed, the tiniest of all
seeds. And it also reminds us of the words of Jesus to his disciples in John 12, in which he compared his own life to a seed
that needed to fall to the earth and die, to be buried, in order
to bloom and bear fruit for the world. Both the hymn and John
12 underscore this important point: in order for fruit to be
born, a seed has to be planted. To rise up, one must go down.

John's Gospel builds the suspense right from the beginning.
It is festival time in Jerusalem. Jesus is there with his disciples,
joined by a huge crowd of people. Not just locals, John says,
but an international event. John says there are Greeks there as
well as Jews.

And it is in this moment that Jesus says, "The time has come
for the Human One to be glorified.

At which point the objective observer might say, "All right! This is it! This is the moment that Jesus is going to rise and be glorified!" If there was any moment for Jesus to shine, to be presented as the King of the Universe, the Lord of all Creation, the Great and Mighty God himself, this would be the time. Let everyone know. Rise up and be made known. The stage is set for a great unveiling.

And yet . . .

Instead of rising up, Jesus says something that utterly shocks the disciples, surprises the reader, and turns conventional wisdom on its ear. He knows full well that if you seek to rise up, you will only tumble down.

And so he says,

> I assure you that unless a grain of wheat falls into the earth and dies, it can only be a single seed. But if it dies, it bears much fruit. Those who love their lives will lose them, and those who hate their lives in this world will keep them forever. Whoever serves me must follow me. Wherever I am, there my servant will also be. My Father will honor whoever serves me. (John 12:24–26)

We want to say, "What? Excuse me Jesus?" That doesn't make sense! Everyone knows that if you want to be great, you have to climb the ladder of success! You have to be better than the next guy! You have to sink the competition! You have to look out for yourself! You have to ascend the promotional and corporate ladder! What is this nonsense about going down and falling to the earth in order to be great?

Jesus says it. If you want to be great, you have to descend. You have to descend into greatness; which, for Jesus, means giving up his life, sacrificing himself.

But Jesus puts it differently. In order for a seed to bloom and bear fruit, it must first be planted in the ground. So if you want to rise up, you must first come down: down to take the form of a servant, down in self-sacrifice, down in giving others' needs their due attention, down in telling others about God. As the hymn suggests, "Give up your strength the seed to nourish."

As we prepare for Christmas along our Advent journey, God calls each of us to live in the example of Christ, which means, first and foremost, to take the form of a servant.

And what a challenge this is for us:

— A challenge to live with the needs of others in mind first, rather than your own.
— A challenge to serve in your church with energy and vitality and not leave it up to others to do the work that you are uniquely equipped and called to perform.
— A challenge to turn your life around, get rid of the bad habits and the obstacles to God's grace that have plagued you for so long.
— A challenge to tell others about Jesus, to let them know about God's love for them, and not let another moment pass by before they have had the opportunity to see their lives transformed the way yours was transformed.
— A challenge to humble yourself and give your life up for God, so that as you, a grain of wheat, fall to the earth, you can rise up and bear fruit.

The challenge is yours if you will seize it. Be strong enough to give up your strength so that the glory of Christ may bloom in your life.

Reflection

What fears do you have related to living a life of self-emptying and self-sacrifice? Which of the above challenges for Advent are easiest for you to consider? Which ones are hardest?

Prayer

God, I confess to you my reluctance to surrender to you in obedience. Remind me of your call on my life, to serve God and others without any desire for glory. Amen.

14

The Power of the Son

Read John 1:1–14

Stars, keep the watch. When night is dim,
    one more light the bowl shall brim,
shining beyond the frosty weather,
    bright as sun and moon together.
People, look east and sing today: Love, the Star, is on the way.
                —*"People, Look East," verse 3*

What came into being
    through the Word was life,
    and the life was the light for all people.
The light shines in the darkness,
    and the darkness doesn't extinguish the light.
                —*John 1:4–5*

In some ways, the Gospel of John and the Epistle of 1 John are easy to get mixed up. There is the obvious connection in the names of these books, but they are also similar in writing style, themes, terminology, and imagery.

In fact, you see this right at the start of the two books:

John: "In the beginning was the Word . . ."

1 John: "We announce to you what existed from the beginning . . . about the word of life."

Right from the start, both books want you to know something that they believe is foundational, absolutely critical, to living. If you don't get this, they would say, nothing else matters. They want you to know who Jesus is.

They take different paths to get there. John is all about belief, right thinking about Jesus Christ. First John is all about ethics, right behavior in response to Jesus. Together, they remind us that both belief and behavior are important. You can't have one without the other.

You see, it is not enough to believe the right things about the Christian faith, to know the key elements of the faith, to "get it" intellectually. All this means very little in the book of 1 John unless you allow it to shape your behavior, your ethics, your way of life.

Belief shapes ethics.

If we believe that Jesus is the one we say he is, then that ought to make a difference in how we behave.

So who is Jesus?

In John, Jesus says, "I am the light of the world." And in 1 John, we hear: "God is light and in him is no darkness at all." Clearly, both John and 1 John would say that Jesus is the light. "This is the message we have heard from him and announce to you," 1 John 1:5 says, " 'God is light and there is no darkness in him at all.'"

This is an image that clearly resonates with the third verse of "People, Look East." It is a verse that seems to leap off the viewfinder of the Hubble telescope, gazing on the vast expanse of the universe and honing in on the stars, the moon, and the sun. Suddenly, the hymn becomes a planetarium full of christological imagery, comparing Jesus to a shining star that lights up the brimming bowl of the galaxy, cutting through the frost of cold weather, and even the heavenly objects we see every day and night: the sun and the moon.

Taken together, the Gospel of John, the Epistle of 1 John, and the third verse of "People, Look East" prompt a comparison between Jesus Christ, son of God, and our own sun, the center of our solar system.

In what ways is Jesus Christ like the sun? How does the light of Jesus, the power of the Son, impact and shape our lives? How does this God who draws near to us in Jesus remove the darkness from our lives?

And how will our belief in that Jesus shape our behavior?

1. The sun is the source of our life. Without the sun, we would have no plants and, therefore, no animals or humans. There would be no life either great or small; nor would there be weather patterns or seasons, no water cycles, of rain and steam. This planet would simply be a lifeless, cold ball of ice. The sun is the source of all life.

Now, if Jesus is the source of your life, then the ethical implication is that you must always be in touch with that source. This means that followers of Christ do not get to choose whether or not they must pray, or read the Scriptures, or gather with other believers. They do not get to choose whether or not to give of their time, talents, and treasures. If you want to tap into the power of the Son, the Son of God, these things are simply not optional.

2. The sun illuminates our world and removes darkness. Imagine a world without light, a world of complete and immense darkness. Imagine how depressing, how scary, how intolerable life would be without daylight in our lives or light of any kind. The sun brightens our dispositions, illuminates our path, and vanquishes the fears and danger of darkness in our world.

Now, if Jesus is the light of the world, then the ethical implication is that you must allow that light to remove the darkness in your life. Perhaps there are things in your life that need to be confessed, for which you need to repent. By God's light revealed in Jesus, you can be forgiven of those sins right now and choose to live a bright new life.

3. The sun gives us direction and gives us a sense of time. We order our time around the sun. We define our years based on our journey around it. We dictate our seasons based on our position in relation to it. We work during the daylight and slumber in its absence. We define our noon hour by the position of the sun in the sky. The sun gives us direction and orders our lives.

Now, if Jesus is the light, then we must reorient our sense of purpose and our sense of time—not around our own needs and perspectives but around the kingdom of God. We must gauge our sense of success by what we do for God, not by what we gain for ourselves. We must see our greatest contributions not in what we keep or possess but in what we create for God that will live long past us. We remember that the impact that we make is not limited to what happens between birth and death; the timeline of God follows a grand, sweeping arc, from eternity to eternity.

4. The sun can be harnessed for its power. Solar power can harness the sun's energy to power our lives. It can heat our homes and power our electronics. The sun can give us power.

And if Jesus is who we believe Jesus is, then we can also tap into that same power of God, to do what we would otherwise deem as impossible: to forgive others for what they have done against us; to be brokers of peace in a time of violence; to overcome our temptations, and to live a new kind of life. This is the promise of Jesus the sun—the Son's—coming into the world.

Reflection

In what ways are you living in darkness right now? What does it mean to you to think of the light of Jesus as a kind of light that illuminates your darkness?

Prayer

Dear God, thank you for refusing to take the easy way out and disregard us in the midst of our darkness. Thank you for your encouragement, nurturing, and love, in the name of our Creator, Redeemer, and Sustainer. Amen.

15

The Return of the King

Read Matthew 25:31–46

Come, thou almighty King,
help us thy name to sing, help us to praise.
Father, all glorious, o'er all victorious,
come, and reign over us, Ancient of Days!
　　　　　—*"Come, Thou Almighty King," verse 1*

"Then the king will reply to them, 'I assure you that when
you have done it for one of the least of these brothers and
sisters of mine, you have done it for me.'"
　　　　　—*Matthew 25:40*

The hymn "Come, Thou Almighty King" is unmistakably clear about its signature description of Jesus. He is the king, the One who rules and reigns in the world and in our hearts, for all eternity.

The idea of Jesus returning to earth as a victorious king has been the source of great speculation over recent centuries of church history. As the twentieth century drew to a close, and the year 2000 drew near, predictions about the exact date of the return of Jesus seemed to reach a fever pitch. The Left Behind books by Jerry B. Jenkins and Tim LaHaye populated the national bestseller lists. Many evangelical televangelists began speaking about signs of the end times, interpreting the troubling headlines of the day as indications that Jesus was coming back. And a poll at the time by *Newsweek* magazine showed that nearly half of Americans—45 percent—believed Jesus would be coming back in the next one thousand years.[1]

So, what do we do about all of this talk of Jesus' second coming?

If you ask the early Christian community, particularly the group to which Matthew's Gospel is written, they would have an interesting response. Matthew alone records the story about the sheep and the goats separated by the judge at the end of time. In this story from Matthew 25, the judge orders that those who cared for Jesus when he was naked, hungry, sick, and imprisoned are welcomed into the kingdom. Those who did not care for Jesus are eternally condemned.

When given this sentence, both groups respond, "Lord, when did we ever experience you in this way?" To which the master says, "When you did it to the least of these, you did it to me."

Matthew's response to the question of Jesus' return is very clear. Don't wait for Jesus to come back someday. Jesus is already here. The return of Jesus is not some future expectation; it is a present reality. Don't be looking up in the sky for a rapturous return, when in fact Christ is already among you, in the faces, stories, and lives of those who are oppressed and downtrodden.

This is the expectation of Advent: to live in the hope of the culmination of human history in the inbreaking of the kingdom through Christ, and to live in the present reality of seeking and doing the work of Christ in our day and time. We live with eyes fixed on the future and hands active in the present. Christ is already here and not yet here.

When speculating on Christ's return, a segment of the Christian church in recent years has focused on the book of Revelation and interpreted this book as strictly future predicting. This is among the most recent ways of looking at Revelation, and it emerged in the nineteenth century, when a preacher named John Nelson Darby developed a theology known as *dispensationalism*. The Left Behind series was written through this lens. Looking at Revelation contextually, however, we see that the community to which Revelation was written was under intense persecution by the Roman Empire. They were people who died as a result of their profession of faith in Christ, who had to meet in seclusion, gather in fear, and live out their commitment as disciples of Christ under penalty of death.

The book of Revelation is filled with veiled language

acknowledging the terror of the empire, naming Caesar, the Roman military, and the government establishment with colorful, dream-like, terrifying language. Over and against this vivid imagery, a simple theme runs throughout the book to the Christian church: Don't give up. Have patience. Endure suffering. Persevere. Hope is coming. Victory will be yours in the end.

Read in that light, the book of Revelation becomes less a book about the end of time and more a word of comfort for us today.

In a time when demonic forces of violence, injustice, and oppression assault us from all sides, when we are tempted to mute our convictions about peace and forgiveness and our prophetic words about justice and social change, the book of Revelation calls the church to hang in there. Don't give up; don't stop being a witness for Jesus, because God will see us through to the end.

What Scripture has to say about Jesus as victorious king, whether in Matthew or Revelation, is that God always sides with the oppressed, and so should we. If it is true that, in Matthew, Jesus is to be found in "the least of these," and if the persecuted church hears a word of comfort about God being on its side, then we must ask ourselves, whose side are we on?

Revelation has a stirring, challenging word for today's church and today's Christians. With whom do you identify more: the persecuted church or the Roman persecutors? Are you in a position of privilege, prestige, self-made power, or are you in the position of self-sacrificial, self-giving love?

Are you on the side of the love of power or on the side of powerless love?

Regardless of how and when Jesus comes back, we are left a mission that constitutes our daily purpose and consumes our daily energies. Our mission is to side with God's activity in the work of the kingdom, reaching out to those desperate, desolate, and deserted. We are called:

— to be a witness for peace in a world full of violence;

—to be agents of forgiveness in a whirlwind of broken relationships;

—to embody love and hope in a world of despair and loneliness;

—to live with the expectation of a soon-to-come king, who in fact is already here.

Reflection

Is there anything liberating or challenging to you about the notion that the "Almighty King" is always on the side of the oppressed? How do you interpret the idea of Christ's returning in final victory?

Prayer

Loving God, thank you for encouraging me to stay hopeful, even in the midst of adversity. Help me to think more about whether I am on your side than whether you are on mine. Amen.

16

What? Me, Holy?

Read 1 Peter 1:3–16

Come, thou incarnate Word,
gird on thy mighty sword, our prayer attend:
Come, and thy people bless, and give thy word success;
Spirit of holiness, on us descend!
— *"Come, Thou Almighty King," verse 2*

Don't be conformed to your former desires, those that
shaped you when you were ignorant. But, as obedient
children, you must be holy in every aspect of your lives, just
as the one who called you is holy. It is written, *You will be
holy, because I am holy.*

— *1 Peter 1:14–16*

The second verse of "Come, Thou Almighty King" is trinitar-
ian in nature. It begins with the second person of the trinity,
the incarnate Word, whom the author portrays with a mighty
sword and attentiveness to prayer. It describes God the Father,
who blesses the people and whose very words create accom-
plishments and success. And it concludes with the Holy Spirit,
who descends on us and imparts holiness.

That last phrase, "Spirit of holiness," is the focus of today's
reflection. And it begins with a quick word association exercise:

What comes to mind when you think of the word *holy?*

It is likely that your first thought is to connect holiness in
relation to God. Fair enough.

But now take it one step further. What comes to mind when
you think of holiness in terms of *people?*

That gets to be more difficult.

You might think of people who are "holier than thou," who
live a kind of ascetic, overly pious, almost Pharisaic life, who
are as out of touch with the real world as they are with any pure
sense of holiness.

You might think of holiness as a goal that is almost impossible to achieve, a kind of mark of excellence that is way out of the realm of possibility for average, ordinary people like most of us.

Or you might think holiness ought to be strictly reserved for describing God. Only God is holy, only God is perfect, wholly just. To call ourselves holy, some think, would be something like blasphemy.

I like the definition of John Brown, the noted Scottish theologian in the nineteenth century, who said, rather simply: "Holiness does not consist in mystic speculations, enthusiastic fervours, or uncommanded austerities; it consists in thinking as God thinks, and willing as God wills."[1]

Holiness is not about a set of standards far out of reach to achieve. Being holy doesn't mean leaving this world for the realms of the ethereal. It simply means being in such an intimate relationship with God that God's motivations become ours, which can then lead to fruitful, righteous, life-giving activities.

But how do we achieve holiness? That is a tempting question to ask, but the truth is, holiness is not something we achieve; for it first involves total surrender. It means allowing our sense of control to be dictated by God and God alone. It does not mean trying to prepare ourselves to be worthy of God; it means resigning ourselves fully to God's authority and God's purposes.

There's a classic sermon illustration told by countless preachers about God's desire in making us holy:

A businessman was once very concerned about his ability to sell a warehouse property he owned. Since he had last surveyed the building, vandals had damaged the doors, smashed the windows, and strewn trash throughout it. The building had been empty for several months, needing repairs because of weather damage and a general lack of maintenance. As the man showed a prospective buyer the building, he took great pains to assure him that he would replace the broken windows, bring in a crew to correct any structural damage, mend the roof, and clean out the garbage. He felt as if he were apologizing at every turn for the condition of the building, but wanted to present the best possible face on the potential sale.

To his surprise, the buyer finally said to him, "Listen, forget about the repairs. I'm going to build something completely different on this land. I don't want the building. I want the site."

Holiness does not mean trying to repair the broken parts of our lives before coming to God. It means surrendering ourselves to God first and allowing God to do that work in us.

First Peter 1:14–16 puts it this way: "Don't be conformed to your former desires, those that shaped you when you were ignorant." Only then does Peter suggest that holiness involves right behavior: "But, as obedient children, you must be holy in every aspect of your lives, just as the one who called you is holy."

Holiness means slowly but steadily trimming back all the things in our lives that should not be there. It means aligning our activities and behaviors in full accordance with God's ways and desires for us.

Listen to these words from John Wesley, founder of the Methodist tradition:

> What, then, is that holiness? It first, through the energy of God, works love to God and all mankind; and, by this love, every holy and heavenly temper, in particular, lowliness, meekness, gentleness, temperance, and longsuffering. (It is) "the keeping (of) the commandments of God; particularly those, "Thou shalt love the Lord thy God with all thy heart, and thy neighbor as thyself." In a word, holiness is the having "the mind that was in Christ," and the "walking as Christ walked."[2]

Holiness, then, is both an identity and an activity. It is a way of being and a way of doing. It involves acknowledging the authority of God and embodying the love of God.

Ultimately, our deepest prayer is that each of us will discover how, in the power of the Holy Spirit, we can grow in an intimate relationship with God that leads us to identify the characteristics of our lives that need to be removed, improved, and reproved.

Reflection

What is your first perception of what the word *holy* means? Is it difficult for you to think of yourself as being called to holiness? How can the coming of Christ help you lead the kind of holy life to which God has called you?

Prayer

God, thank you for calling me to holiness. I pray that you will continue to help me in my journey so that I may offer the fullest and best fulfillment of your will in my life. Amen.

17

Be the Gift

Read Isaiah 40:1–11

Come, holy Comforter,
thy sacred witness bear in this glad hour.
Thou who almighty art, now rule in every heart,
and ne'er from us depart, Spirit of power.
— *"Come, Thou Almighty King," verse 3*

Comfort, comfort my people!
   says your God.
Speak compassionately to Jerusalem,
   and proclaim to her that her compulsory service has ended,
   that her penalty has been paid,
   that she has received from the LORD's hand double for all her sins!
— *Isaiah 40:1–2*

The final verse of the hymn focuses squarely on the work of the Holy Spirit as the source of our comfort, whose sacred witness rules in every heart, and who never departs from us. This theme of comfort connects to the Scripture text from Isaiah, one of the classic Scriptures of Advent. In this passage the prophet gives words of strength to people struggling in exile, reminding them that their penalty has been paid, their sentence will soon be over, and they will receive compassion from God.

Both the hymn and the Isaiah text are very clear in their messages of hope for people of Advent. And I don't know about you, but I find it hard to read the words of Isaiah 40 without hearing the opening recitative of George Frideric Handel's timeless oratorio *Messiah*.

Before the age of thirty, the German-born composer had already achieved superstar, celebrity status as one of the most noted composers and conductors in all of Europe. He composed for famous Italian patrons and notable German theaters and eventually was employed by England's King George I. He was London's most notable and accomplished composer, and he was considered the most important musical influence in the entire baroque period.

By the time he was fifty-four, Handel's life had turned from superstar celebrity to bankrupt pauper. He was depressed. He was suffering from physical ailments, including rheumatism. The shine on his star had faded, his fortunes were depleted, and he was looking ahead to spending the rest of his life in debtor's prison. George Frideric Handel would have been a perfect candidate for an episode of *E! True Hollywood Story*.

And then, two letters arrived. The first was from the Duke of Devonshire, who requested that Handel offer his services to, of all things, a benefit concert for charity. Despite his celebrated past, a dejected, desperate Handel took the gig. He was charged with composing a work that would be performed in the Irish capital of Dublin to benefit several jails, Mercer's Hospital in Stephen Street, and the Charitable Infirmary on the Inn's Quay.

The second letter arrived shortly thereafter. It was from an English landowner named Charles Jennens, an eccentric sort of gentleman who had attempted to write lyrics for Handel in the past. But this time was surprising. Instead of original lyrics, Jennens sent Handel excerpts from the Old Testament, short passages of Scripture about the coming and expectation of Jesus Christ, such as Isaiah 40:

> The voice of him that crieth in the wilderness, Prepare ye the way of the LORD, make straight in the desert a highway for our God. (v. 3 KJV)

And then, the inspiration swept through Handel like a flood. In just seven days, part 1 of his new oratorio was complete. In less than a month, the entire work was complete, and Handel's *Messiah* was born.

It debuted in Dublin in 1742, and it has been debuting in the hearts and minds of countless Advent travelers ever since.

What was it about these passages, such as today's Isaiah reading, that transformed and inspired Handel the way they did?

Surely, this was not the first time he read them. He had known about Jesus and read these Bible passages countless times. But there was something unique about the timing of this reading.

First, he had hit rock bottom. He had acknowledged his desperation and hunger for salvation and freedom from his condition.

Second, add the reality that Handel was being asked to give of himself for charity, for the benefit of his community and people in need. He had likely been asked before to compose for charity, but this may have been the first time he was asked to do so while he himself was a person in need. He was like one beggar telling another beggar where to find bread.

And third, this was a chance to tell others about the hope, the promise, the passion, and the triumph of the story of Jesus. And it was a story he needed to hear as well.

All three points converged in Handel's life to produce a work that would transform the entire musical world and even the world of faith.

Ask yourself, how many times have you heard the stories of Jesus during this Advent time? If you're like me, you can practically recite from memory the key narratives of the Bible, since we have known these stories from childhood. So what in the world might be different about hearing these stories now as opposed to in the past?

Maybe, as Handel discovered, it is not that these stories are different but that *we* are:

We, too, can acknowledge the depths of our hunger and longing.

We, too, can receive the words of Scripture and make them our own.

We, too, can give ourselves—not just our presents—over to acts of love and peace.

It's not about getting gifts. It's not even about giving gifts. It's not about finding the perfect gift for that person who has everything. It's not about giving presents with the hope of pleasing. It's not about throwing the perfect party and making things just right. It's not about giving gifts.

It is about *being* a gift. It is about becoming that gift for the world, the embodiment of God's love for people who need to experience it.

At the heart of the Christmas story, and in the center of the Christian faith, is the incarnation. When God chose to reveal most fully God's love for all creation, God did not purchase a gift and give it to us. God became the gift. God assumed the full likeness and expression of that very same hungry, lonely, sorrowful humanity that God wanted to save.

God's presence was fully made real in the life of a human being, to be our comfort in times of need.

Is it possible God wants to use you and me to be an incarnate gift to comfort someone in need as well?

Reflection

When have you done an act of service for someone else, only to be the one touched by the experience? How might you be the gift for someone else this season?

Prayer

Gracious God, in Jesus, you became a gift for all humanity. Inspire me to become a gift for someone else, without expectation of thanks or repayment. Amen.

18

Choose or Refuse

Read Revelation 3:20

Come, thou long-expected Jesus, born to set the people free;
from our fears and sins release us, let us find our rest in thee.
Israel's strength and consolation, hope of all the earth thou art;
dear desire of every nation, joy of every longing heart.
—*"Come, Thou Long-Expected Jesus," verse 1*

Look! I'm standing at the door and knocking. If any hear my
voice and open the door, I will come in to be with them, and
will have dinner with them, and they will have dinner with me.
—*Revelation 3:20*

The hymn "Come, Thou Long-Expected Jesus" describes
the inner stirrings of a person who desires to find new life in
Christ. With vivid phrases such as "from our fears and sins
release us" and "joy of every longing heart," this hymn is an
accurate description of anyone who longs to experience a new
awakening to the power of God revealed in Jesus Christ. It
speaks of the potential for dramatic rebirth in a person who
chooses to follow Jesus.

Just ask Freeborn Garrettson.

You may not recognize the name Freeborn Garrettson,
unless you were a Methodist living in eighteenth-century America. Born in Maryland, Garrettson became an itinerant Methodist preacher in 1775, at the age of twenty-three. As conflict
brewed in the American colonies with Mother England during
the early days of the Revolutionary War, Garrettson developed
both strong pacifist and antislavery stances, for which he would
be persecuted. Serving primarily in the New York state area,
Garrettson eventually became one of the most important pre-
siding elders of the early Methodist Episcopal Church.

But his story almost didn't unfold that way. Garrettson did
his best to avoid Methodist church meetings early in his life,

as he was fiercely loyal to his roots in the Church of England. But eventually he tired of worship services in which "we had a smooth, moral sermon read, which did not disturb the consciences of any." His experiences in a few Methodist church meetings were quite different; he noted how "the law was thundered down on the hearers and the plan of salvation pointed out." Nevertheless, Garrettson continued to prefer a comfortable faith, which was neither threatened nor threatening.

This would change. On one occasion, he met a man he described as a "zealous Methodist exhorter" who asked Garrettson if he was born again. He told him that he hoped that he was.

"Do you know that your sins are forgiven?" the man asked Garrettson.

"I do not," he responded, "neither do I believe that there is such a knowledge to be had in this world."

This conversation would continue to haunt Garrettson until a moment when he experienced an internally audible voice from God, saying to him, "I have come once more to make you an offer of salvation, and it is the last time. Choose or refuse."

Garrettson describes his response:

I verily did believe that, if I rejected that offer, mercy would be clean gone forever. Heaven and hell were disclosed to my interior eye, and life and death were set before me. I was surrounded as it were by a divine power and shaken over hell. I saw clearly that pride and unbelief had kept me from God. It was like giving up the ghost. I was perfectly reconciled with the justice of God for I never could before now be reconciled to that attribute. I threw down my bridle on my horse's neck and lifted my hands and eyes to heaven and cried out, "Lord, I submit, make me as thou wouldst have me to be." I know the moment when every false prop was taken away, and I reconciled to be the plan of salvation by Jesus Christ. I could look up and see by an eye of faith the great Jehovah reconciled through Jesus Christ to my poor soul. This power was attended with peace and joy in so much that I seemed to be all taken up with Jesus, and although all alone in a solitary mood, in the dead time of night, I could but lift up my voice and praise God aloud so that I might have been heard a far off. Now it was that I saw the way of salvation and knew that my sins were forgiven.[1]

Freeborn Garrettson was a changed man. After many years of growing up with a version of the Christian faith that was lax and neutral, he came to realize that a deeply radical commitment to Christ demanded full confession of his sins and an ongoing desire to follow Jesus with his whole being. As soon as he came to that realization, he lifted his life in praise to God. And as a result, the Methodist renewal movement gained a powerful voice.

Garrettson's new commitment was stirred when he finally acknowledged the deep longing within his soul for a Jesus who had come to release him from his fears and sins and in whom he could find rest. His conversion resonantly echoes the sentiment of the first verse of "Come, Thou Long Expected Jesus," which names Christ as the hope of the whole earth, the desire of every nation, and the joy of every longing heart.

Conversion experiences like that of Freeborn Garrettson are common in the Bible and in the history of the church. But today, these experiences seem to be more the exception than the norm. What prevents people from opening themselves with this kind of humility to a God who yearns to love and forgive them?

And to put it more personally, what is preventing you from acknowledging those barriers that block the free flow of God's grace and love from flowing through you?

Reflection

What would it mean to make this prayer of Freeborn Garrettson your Advent prayer? "Lord, I submit; make me as thou wouldst have me to be"?

Prayer

God, thank you for reaching through the barriers that I have erected that keep me from you. Help me to submit fully to your grace so that I might experience the fullness of your love. Amen.

19

Hopefully

Read 1 Thessalonians 4:13–20

Born thy people to deliver, born a child and yet a king,
born to reign in us forever, now thy gracious kingdom bring.
By thine own eternal Spirit rule in all our hearts alone;
by thine all sufficient merit raise us to thy glorious throne.
—*"Come, Thou Long-Expected Jesus," verse 2*

Brothers and sisters, we want you to know about people who
have died so that you won't mourn like others who don't
have any hope.
—*1 Thessalonians 4:13*

Hope is one of Advent's recurring themes. The biblical substance of hope is summarized beautifully in the second verse of "Come, Thou Long-Expected Jesus." It begins with the human condition, portraying humanity as being in need of deliverance. It speaks of the incarnation of Jesus, capturing both the humanity ("child") and divinity ("king") of Christ. It sweeps into the future, envisioning the rule and reign of Christ in the kingdom of "thy glorious throne."

There is a lot of hope in this hymn and in the season of Advent.

Hopefully, we can sing it. We can sing it hopefully.

There was some interesting news a few years ago when the *Associated Press Stylebook*, the longtime, self-avowed guardian of proper journalistic grammar and word usage, finally relented on a decades-long battle over one of our most common and—they would argue—most misappropriated words.

"Hopefully, you will appreciate this style update, announced at #aces2012," the *AP Stylebook* tweeted on April 17, 2012. "We now support the modern usage of *hopefully*: it's hoped, we hope."[1]

For years, language purists have argued that use of the adverb *hopefully* is suitable only when describing the action of the person in the sentence, when performed in a hopeful manner. As in, "The little boy hopefully tossed his coin into the wishing well." Or, "The girl blew out her birthday candles hopefully." It is about the hope felt by the main character, the subject of the sentence.

But over time, we have expanded its application to include not just the subject of the sentence but also the narrator. "Hopefully, the team will make it to the playoffs," says less about the hope the team feels and more about the person writing the statement. "Hopefully, the two sides can come to an agreement," describes our hopes for the best outcome rather than the emotional state of either party. In other words, we've taken the word *hopefully* and used it as a mirror to reflect our own feelings.

Hopefully, you can see the difference.

When the *AP Stylebook* agreed to this expanded usage, it felt like a defeat for those who have long complained about the ongoing twisting and warping of our English language. It's vagabonds like us, they would say, who butcher perfectly good words, such as *hopefully*, and cast its carcass on the wreckage of debates over words such as nauseated vs. nauseous and healthy vs. healthful.

However, for Advent pilgrims like us, this news reinforces what we should already know. This is not just a season for third-person hope. It is more than just remembering the main characters in the Christmas pageant. Yes, we sense the hopeful anticipation in Mary's heart, and the hopeful obedience that marked Joseph's spirit. We remember the hopeful word of the angels who broke through with amazing news to the shepherds, and the hope that was born and wrapped in manger hay.

But this is also about the hope we might find for ourselves. The second verse of "Come, Thou Long Expected Jesus" names the hope deep within us for a God who would be born anew into the world: born to deliver us, born to be a king, born to reign forever, born to usher in a new kingdom. And it is a hope that this Jesus would fill the deepest parts of our existence, "in all our hearts alone," to cleanse us from our sin and heal us of our brokenness.

When we light the Advent candles, when we gaze on the twinkling star lights on our Chrismon trees, when we pause during our busy days and refocus our attention on the God who leads us on our journeys, then hopefully, hopefully, we become people of hope ourselves.

This is not simply a time of fondly recollecting stories from long ago; it's also an invitation to allow those stories to sort through and soothe our conflicted lives so that the hope that God offers can become our own. For whatever reason you are in need of hope today, may God's richest promises and possibilities come to you and those you love.

Let us, then, be full of hope.

Reflection

How might the story of Jesus' birth give you a sense of hope, to "sort through and soothe" your conflicted life? How can you be a source of hope for someone else today?

Prayer

Eternal God, you are the source of all hope. You give me reason to look forward when I am stuck in the past and troubled by the present. Grant me the strength and the patience to hope. Amen.

20

Called to Do Better

Read Mark 1:1–8

All earth is waiting to see the Promised One,
and the open furrows, the sowing of the Lord.
All the world, bound and struggling, seeks true liberty;
it cries out for justice and searches for the truth.
—"Toda la Tierra," *verse 1**

John was in the wilderness calling for people to be baptized
to show that they were changing their hearts and lives and
wanted God to forgive their sins. Everyone in Judea and all
the people of Jerusalem went out to the Jordan River and
were being baptized by John as they confessed their sins.
—*Mark 1:4–5*

The Spanish hymn *"Toda La Tierra"* (known in English as "All Earth Is Waiting") begins with a macroscopic view of the planet, as if gazing on the earth from space. This wide-angle view of the world gives us a new perspective on the ailments of the human condition, and the first verse of the hymn contains just that kind of diagnosis. It speaks of a world that is waiting for hope, "bound and struggling," and crying out for justice.

It is the perspective that a certain astronaut considered on January 10, 2011. That day, soaring 250 miles above the earth, the commander of the International Space Station spoke to the world. Flight controllers in Houston fell hushed, listening to each carefully crafted word:

> As I look out the window, I see a very beautiful planet that seems very inviting and peaceful. Unfortunately, it is not. These days, we are constantly reminded of the unspeakable acts of violence and damage we can inflict upon one another, not just with our actions, but also with our irresponsible words. We're better than this. We must do better.[1]

These poignant words were uttered by astronaut Scott Kelly, who during that week was notable for more than just his endeavors in orbit. He is also the brother-in-law of Arizona Representative Gabrielle Giffords, one of the victims of a tragic shooting in Tucson, Arizona, on Saturday, January 8, 2011. Though his vantage point afforded him a placid, serene view of the planet, Commander Kelly was not distant enough to escape the cold, harsh realities of a world fractured by violence, hatred, and suffering. He could see, as in the words of the hymn, that "all the earth was waiting" for a peace to end the violence.

Indeed, the shocking event that killed six and injured thirteen was a vivid reminder to all of us of the brokenness of the human condition. The following day, churches around the world gathered around their baptismal fonts to observe Baptism of the Lord Sunday. As members of my congregation stood to reaffirm the vows we received at our own baptism, I was struck by the following words: "Do you accept the freedom and power God gives you to resist evil, injustice, and oppression in whatever forms they present themselves?"[2]

Most of the time, the words of our liturgy are precise, economical, and direct. But the power of this particular vow is in its open-endedness. When we talk about wrestling against evil, injustice, and oppression, we aren't talking about children's sermon sins or Sunday school foibles. We are talking about forces that don't conform to our preconceived notions and are subtle enough to sneak into our communal conscience. They present themselves as if they have a life and mind of their own, like a serpent emerging from a garden's shadows. They appear in many different forms, which means we have to be diligent and sober, determined to unmask them. While we'd prefer to view humanity from the safety of the skies, we are called to holy investigation, to expose the evils, injustices, and oppressions that run rampant throughout the world.

This is one reason John the Baptist is such an important fixture in our Advent journey. He tells us to get ready for the coming of Christ by drawing us to the waters of baptism. For it is to the ancient and sacred symbol of water that the people of

God have always turned to be reminded of God's presence and power, and to surrender in obedience to its power to cleanse and purify our sins.

Through baptism, we have the freedom and power to resist the evils of hateful and polarizing rhetoric from either extreme of the political spectrum. Words that leave the realm of earnest debate and thoughtful disagreement and put lives at risk have no place in our society, let alone in the kingdom of God.

Of course, in the end, the shooter in Tucson must fully assume blame for his diabolical act of wickedness. But any of us who call ourselves Christians and are claimed by God in our baptisms cannot sit back passively with a space-station perspective while the world spirals in sin. Simply put, our baptism will not allow us this option. We have no choice but to resist.

Yes, in the words of Commander Scott Kelly, "we can do better than this." We do not need to sit idly by while a world filled with evil, injustice, and oppression suffers senseless tragedy. The church is called by God to embody the message and vision of Jesus Christ and to carry hope to a hurting world. We have the freedom and power to make it happen, and it is work we must do.

Our baptism will not allow us to do otherwise. And neither will our preparations for Advent.

Reflection

Have you ever thought about your baptism as a reminder of your call and qualification to resist evil, injustice, and oppression? Does that understanding change your response to tragic events? How might you begin to help the world "do better" and build God's kingdom on earth?

Prayer

Eternal God, thank you for sending your Son Jesus, whose life, death, and resurrection conquered evil and sin. May his life be a model to us of the power of your grace and love, and may it empower us to build your kingdom on earth. Amen.

21

Emmanuel

Read Matthew 1:18–23

Thus says the prophet to those of Israel,
"A virgin mother will bear Emmanuel,"
for his name is "God with us," our brother shall be,
with him hope will blossom once more within our hearts.
— *"Toda la Tierra," verse 2**

Now all of this took place so that what the Lord had spoken
through the prophet would be fulfilled:
   Look! A virgin will become pregnant and give birth to a son,
   And they will call him, Emmanuel.
(*Emmanuel* means "God with us.")

—*Matthew 1:22–23*

The second verse of *"Toda La Tierra"* introduces us to one
of the most important and prevalent names for Jesus in the
Advent story. It is a name that is both descriptive and predic-
tive, as it describes both the nature of God revealed in Jesus
and the promise of God's work among us through Jesus. In the
name *Emmanuel,* we hear that God is with us, calling Jesus our
brother and promising a hope that will blossom in our hearts.

It is appropriate, then, to turn our attention to the passage
in the Advent narrative that gives us the origin of that name, in
a story that involves one of the great characters in the Gospels.

Over and against the good cheer and bright lights of our
culture's Christmas observances, Matthew's Gospel breaks into
our society's regularly scheduled holiday programming with
this breaking news: the world we live in is broken. The other
Gospel writers use different perspectives to tell us about the
birth of Jesus, but Matthew is unique: No shepherds, no visit
of the angel to Mary, no angelic choirs, no "Glory to God in
the Highest," and nothing that you would normally associate
with most kids' Christmas pageants.

*©1972, 1993 Centre De Pastoral Liturgica. Administered by OCP, 5536 NE Hassalo,
Portland, OR 97213. All rights reserved. Used with permission.

Instead, Matthew paints a picture of a world gripped by chaos, confusion, and disillusionment. So it's no wonder that Matthew chooses to spend time fleshing out one of the most important characters in the birth narrative, someone who often gets the supporting-role treatment: Meet Joseph, father of Jesus.

Our introduction to the father of Jesus is a far cry from the way we meet the mother of Jesus in Luke. Luke renders a beautiful story of the angel's visit to Mary, and we hear her croon a beautiful song about her soul magnifying the Lord; in Matthew there is no peaceful visit to Joseph but rather a story of scandal, stress, and social stigma.

Joseph hears about Mary's pregnancy, remembers that most baby-making kits require two people for assembly, and realizes that no one in town is going to believe them when he tells them that Mary was impregnated by the Holy Spirit, not by him or any other man.

In other words, Joseph knows that his culture is addicted to scandals, to tabloids, to gossip, and to rumor mills. And he knows that if such news were to break out into the world, it would essentially mean a death sentence for his beloved Mary. That is how much the world of Jesus was addicted to violence and quick to shed blood. Even in the name of religious devotion, people were quick to be bloodthirsty.

And that's just chapter 1 of Matthew. In the next chapter, we get to the chief symbol for all that is power hungry and loveless in the world: a king named Herod, who was so paranoid about his grip on power that he ordered the massacre of all boys under the age of two—a massive holocaust of innocent children that we are horrified to even think about.

You see, in Matthew's Christmas story, it's not such a wonderful life after all, despite what the popular Christmas movie might say. Instead, Matthew paints a picture of a world so deluded by power, so soaked with blood, so prone to violence and addicted to revenge, that we wonder why in the world anyone would want to bring a child into that kind of world.

In other words, it's not unlike the world we live in today.

I don't know about you, but there is something truly

incongruous about hearing songs that say, "It's the Most Wonderful Time of the Year" when so many of our kids in this country go to bed hungry at night. It's hard to sing "Have Yourself a Merry Little Christmas" when we know that for many families in communities across the country, there will be one less gift under the tree and one less child at the Christmas dinner table because a loved one was murdered. It's hard to sing "Joy to the World" when the world is full of communities struggling under the whir of bullets and bombs and scraping together livelihoods in the wake of natural disasters.

Matthew wrote his Gospel so that we wouldn't forget what kind of world we really live in and so that we would remember just exactly why we need Jesus to come into this world in the first place. Matthew reminds us of the prophet Isaiah's words, the proclamation of Emmanuel.

It's the name that the angel told Joseph to give to Jesus in that same dream, and it means "God with us." I love that it came to Joseph in a dream. In the midst of our nightmares, in the midst of our darkness, in the midst of the horror of the way the world is today, God still speaks in a dream. It's a dream that comes in the form of a vision, a vision that is captured in a single name: Emmanuel. No matter what you are going through in this world, no matter how bad it seems, and no matter how awful it may still get, there is this truth: God is with us.

And that is the best news of all.

Reflection

Consider the meaning of *Emmanuel*. What difference does it make in your life to remember that God is with you? How might it help you model the obedience of Joseph?

Prayer

God, thank you for the life of Joseph. Help me to live with that same kind of surrender and obedience to your will, regardless of the cost. Amen.

22

The Gift of Silence

Read Luke 1:5–25, 57–80

Lo, how a rose e'er blooming from tender stem hath sprung,
of Jesse's lineage coming, by faithful prophets sung.
It came, a flower bright, amid the cold of winter,
when half spent was the night.
> —*"Lo, How a Rose E'er Blooming," verse 1*

After asking for a tablet, he surprised everyone by writing,
"His name is John." At that moment, Zechariah was able to
speak again, and he began praising God.
> —*Luke 1:63–64*

In the opening verse to the beautiful Advent hymn "Lo, How
a Rose E'er Blooming," we see a beautiful and peculiar phrase
that describes the ancestors of our faith: "Of Jesse's lineage
coming as those of old have sung." And in the story of Advent,
one particular man of old sang of the coming of the promised
one of Jesse's lineage. But he was not able to come to that place
of singing until he learned to incorporate silence in his life.

A few years ago, I lost my voice. It was in the middle of a
production run of *A Christmas Carol: The Musical,* performed
by my local community theater, in which I had a fairly prom-
inent singing role. After over-singing and straining to hit the
high notes, I was pretty much unable to talk, and for a few
days I wasn't sure if I'd be able to sing my song and perform
my role on stage. There obviously was quite a bit of anxiety on
my part, wondering whether I'd be able to talk again, let alone
sing and preach.

I tried everything. Steam-breathing treatments, hot tea,
throat lozenges, water. My administrative assistant cooked up
some awful concoction involving lemon juice and cider vinegar
that was amazingly nasty. And sure enough, when I arrived in
the office one morning, she had a cup of it and made me drink

it. The terrible drink did its trick, however: it successfully kept me from coming in to the office so I wouldn't have to drink any more of it, which meant that I stayed home, away from people, and rested my voice in the quiet of my house.

Quiet—silence, rest—was the surefire and only true cure for my overworked vocal chords.

So it is with you: The best remedy for your overworked and overwrought soul is silence, prayer, and quiet time with God. And if you can do that, you will experience great healing.

Just ask Zechariah.

Zechariah was a religious leader, a priest in the temple. One day, while doing his priestly duties, he was visited by an angel: Gabriel.

The angel said to Zechariah, "Don't be afraid, Zechariah. Your prayers have been heard. Your wife Elizabeth will give birth to your son, and you must name him John" (Luke 1:13).

Despite this amazing news, Zechariah doubted. His soul was troubled. His soul was confused. His soul was—well, a lot like ours. He said, "How can I be sure of this? My wife and I are very old" (v. 18).

I'm not sure why Zechariah doubted, but he did.

So, God did something to Zechariah. Because of his words, God struck him mute. Gabriel said,

> "I am Gabriel. I stand in God's presence. I was sent to speak to you and to bring this good news to you. Know this: What I have spoken will come true at the proper time. But because you didn't believe, you will remain silent, unable to speak until the day when these things happen." (vv. 19–20)

Now, it's possible to interpret God's actions here as punishment. You could look at the severity of this and say it happened because God was angry. But I think there's another explanation. It was a gift to Zechariah.

Zechariah needed to be quiet. He needed nine months to hear nothing but his own thoughts and the words of others. He needed to quiet his life and let silence fill him. He was not ready to hear the good news because his life was too noisy. He was not ready to sing the song of hope because his lips were singing songs of doubt, songs of despair, songs of uncertainty. So for nine months, Zechariah could not speak.

As Elizabeth's womb got larger, Zechariah could not speak words of anticipation.

As she went into labor, he could not offer words of comfort.

As she gave birth to the promised child, Zechariah could not rejoice with their family and friends.

Zechariah had a lot of time to think and reflect.

The day came when the child was to be named and circumcised. The neighbors all thought the child should be named after his father: Zech Jr., maybe, or "Little Z." But Elizabeth said, "No." He should be called John, the named prescribed by the angel.

"But no one in your family is called John," they said. "What kind of name is John?"

And then, Zechariah, communicating with only a stylus and a writing tablet, wrote the words. "His name is John." Zechariah finally got it. He understood the angel's words. He accepted the promise into his life. He was ready to profess it before others. The nine months of silence had worked.

At that moment, his throat was opened, his lips could speak, and he could sing a song of hope with everyone.

If Zechariah's story offers a lesson to us, what might it be? I think it reminds us that there is value in silence.

If Zechariah were alive, he would give us this simple advice: Quiet your life, and hear the song. The song of hope starts as a faint whisper but ends with reverberant praise. This song can be too quickly drowned out by worldly noise and ignored by human doubts. This song is for the world to hear and for you to sing.

Reflection

Does your perception of Zechariah's nine months of silence change when you think of it as a prescription from God rather than a sentence from God? How might you begin to incorporate more silence into your life during the remainder of this Advent season and beyond?

Prayer

God, silence all voices but yours. Train me to focus on your words so that I might hear your guidance and encouragement in my life. Amen.

23

God's Answer to Suffering

Read Isaiah 64:1–4

Isaiah 'twas foretold it, the rose I have in mind;
with Mary we behold it, the virgin mother kind.
To show God's love aright she bore for us a Savior,
when half spent was the night.
          —*"Lo, How a Rose E'er Blooming," verse 2*

If only you would tear open the heavens and come down!
Mountains would quake before you
like fire igniting brushwood or making water boil.
If you would make your name known to your enemies,
the nations would tremble in your presence.
          —*Isaiah 64:1–2*

The second verse of "Lo, How a Rose E'er Blooming" paints a metaphorical picture of the arrival of Jesus as coming when "half spent was the night." Perhaps we can interpret that phrase literally, such that the hymn suggests that Jesus was born in the middle of the night. Alternatively, we might consider the "night" to be the condition of human suffering, and the hymn therefore becomes a reminder that Jesus was born not to help us escape our suffering but as an answer to our suffering, calling us when our hope is "half spent."

In Walter Isaacson's book chronicling the life of Steve Jobs, he relays a story from Jobs's adolescence. Jobs's parents wanted him to be raised in the Christian faith, so they started attending a Lutheran church with some regularity. At age thirteen, Jobs went to see the Lutheran pastor, and in his hand was the latest cover of *Life* magazine, from July 12, 1969. On the cover were two starving children, victims of the ongoing war in Biafra, against Nigeria.

He asked the pastor, "If I hold up my fingers, does God know how many fingers I'm about to hold up?" And the pastor said, "Yes, God knows everything." Then Jobs showed the pastor the cover. "Then does God know about this, and what's going to happen to these children?"

The pastor stammered around with some answers: yes, God knows. We don't understand that kind of thing. Then Jobs announced that he didn't want to have anything to do with any kind of religion that believes in a God like that. And he never stepped foot in a church again.[1]

These are difficult questions, of course, and the problems of suffering and evil in the world are, for many people, the single greatest obstacle to faith. Like so many people in times of trouble, we wonder why God doesn't just show up and fix things. We cry out, wishing that God would!

As the prophet Isaiah prayed:

> If only you would tear open the heavens and come down!
> Mountains would quake before you
> like fire igniting brushwood or making water boil.
> If you would make your name known to your enemies,
> the nations would tremble in your presence.
>
> (Isa. 64:1–2)

Theologians and philosophers have wrestled with how a good and powerful God could allow such atrocities to exist. But an even less complicated question exists for which there are equally elusive answers: Why does the church allow such suffering and evil to exist?

The question for you and I today ought to be, in the face of such hardship and suffering faced by so many in the world today, why does the church allow these things to happen?

We can rest assured that in Jesus' mind, there was no debate, no confusion about the answer. When Jesus uttered the very first foundational message about the nature, mission, and purpose of the church—"I tell you that you are Peter. And I'll build my church on this rock"— he also gave this amazing image: "The gates of the underworld won't be able to stand against it" (Matt. 16:18).

See, we often think of the church as a congregation, huddled together on a Sunday morning, while the influences of the world are all around us: vying for our time and our energy, tempting us and threatening us. That's the exact opposite of what Jesus had in mind for the mission of the church. He said that when the church is doing its job, the "gates of the underworld won't be able to stand against it." In other words, the church is always supposed to go on the offensive against hell, not stand passively, defensively against it. It's to be like a battering ram, beating down the doors anywhere you can find hell in the world today.

And where is hell? Anywhere God's love is not being fully experienced.

Anywhere a child suffers because of malnutrition, there is hell.

Anywhere a family shivers in the cold because they cannot afford warm clothing during the winter, there is hell.

Anywhere a person is addicted to alcohol or drugs or sex or gambling or any pleasure—full force, beyond their control—there is hell.

Anywhere a marriage breaks because of betrayal or guilt, there is hell.

Anywhere a corporation builds a fortune on the backs of the poor, there is hell.

Anywhere a country is savaged by war, there is hell.

Anywhere an adult can't read or get a job or have access to quality health care—through no fault of his or her own—there is hell.

And wherever there is hell, in the vision of Jesus, there ought to be the church, beating down its doors, because its gates cannot stand against it. Our job as a church is nothing short of putting hell out of business.

You see, whenever the mission and message of God's kingdom wants to break through, into the misery and suffering and brokenness of creation, then the gates of hell tremble and quake and ultimately cannot stand.

So, ultimately, the question about suffering and evil does not have to be, "What is God doing about people who are suffering?" The question is, "What are *we* doing about it? What are *you* doing about it?"

Reflection

What sort of "night" do you see in the world around you? Have you ever identified with the kind of struggle that Steve Jobs related to the minister? What does it mean to you that Jesus was born into a dark and suffering world?

Prayer

Eternal God, thank you for not leaving us alone in our suffering. Give me a more vital sense of your presence in the midst of my darkness, and empower me to be an agent of healing and peace for others. Amen.

24

Personal, Not Digital

Read Luke 2:1–7

This flower, whose fragrance tender with sweetness fills the air,
dispel with glorious splendor the darkness everywhere.
Enfleshed, yet very God, from sin and death he save us
and lightens every load.
— *"Lo, How a Rose E'er Blooming," verse 3*

While they were there, the time came for Mary to have her
baby. She gave birth to her firstborn child, a son, wrapped him
snugly, and laid him in a manger, because there was no place
for them in the guestroom.
— *Luke 2:6–7*

Then the angel said to the shepherds, "Do not be afraid; I am
bringing you good news by e-mail and text message. You can
visit his Facebook page and follow him on Twitter. Be sure to
check out his new website and download his iPhone App . . ."

Neuroscientist Gary Small has studied the effects that this
vast array of digital technologies has on the human brain. With
every moment spent on the internet, e-mail, smartphones, and
other digital devices, our brains are literally being rewired,
through complex biochemical and neural reactions.

There are a few physiological benefits. Hand-eye coordi-
nation can improve, as well as the ability to multitask. There
are also harmful effects. Changes in the dorsolateral prefron-
tal cortex—the part of our brains responsible for decision
making—make us less able to focus on one task at a time,
diminish our short-term memory, and produce a state of
"continuous partial attention," in which we find it more
difficult to spend a prolonged time in patient, thoughtful
contemplation.[1]

Despite our new abilities to communicate efficiently with
more people at the same time, our rewired brains also make
it harder for us to deeply and intimately connect with people

one-on-one. We become unable to recognize subtle meaning in a person's facial expressions, to be fully present with them in conversation. We lose the "personal touch."

And most disturbing of all, Dr. Small has discovered that our hippocampus—the part of our brains that, among other things, determines feelings of self-esteem and self-worth—is gradually shrinking. This explains what many describe as "brain strain" or "digital fog" after spending long hours with their digital devices. We feel irritable, lonely, tired, and of general low self-worth.

Now pardon the utter irony in the fact that I discovered Dr. Small's findings while perusing the web, in an article from a recent issue of *Scientific American Mind* ("Your iBrain: How Technology Changes the Way We Think").[2]

I offer this caution to myself as much as to anyone else. As a forty-something Gen-Xer, I was among the first generation to grow up in the digital culture. I am as big a techie as the next person: with my laptop computer, wi-fi access, iPhone, tablet, and cable television.

I think this all points to another way to prepare for and appreciate what God did through Jesus Christ. When God chose to offer an ultimate revelation to humanity, God did not choose another written edict or another cryptic message hidden in creation for us to decipher. God chose a personal, one-on-one encounter, spending time with us, experiencing life as one of us, the Creator becoming creation.

God chose the incarnation, and we called him, "God with Us." This is captured by the verse in today's hymn, "Lo, How a Rose E'er Blooming," which describes Jesus as "true man, yet very God." It gives witness to the Word made flesh, who chose to connect with us in the most personal, least digital, least hypothetical way. In Jesus, God's love became real, in the form of a human who was very much human and very much divine.

Maybe there's a lesson here for all of us brain-strained, digitally fogged creatures about the importance of being present and personal with one another, just as God did for us.

—It might mean checking email only a few times a day. Put the computer away at night. Set aside your smartphone. Convince yourself of the truth that you're not really as important as you think you are.

—Remember that family dinner table? Put it to good use again, and remind your kids what it means to interact with someone face-to-face.

—The next time you think about sending an e-mail, try making a call instead. If possible, pay a personal visit and look the person in the eye. Try actually handwriting a note, with your own hand, and putting it in an envelope you seal yourself.

—Read an actual book that you hold with your hands, or a newspaper that you peruse with your own fingers.

That dusty book of chapters and verses sitting unused in your house? Open it up. Reading the written Word is the best way to get to know the Word Made Flesh, one-on-one, face-to-face. Spend some time, distraction-free, focusing only on this God who went to great lengths to draw near to you. It's time to return the favor.

Reflection

What do you think of Dr. Small's assessment of the effects of digital technology on us? Do you see any of those symptoms in your life? How can you be more present to those around you this season and in the coming year?

Prayer

Ever-Present God, thank you for choosing to come to earth to be among us. Thank you for the way the incarnation of Jesus reminds us to be an incarnate presence for others. Empower us to live into that vision so that we might make your love real to others. Amen.

25

She Said Yes

Read Luke 1:26–38

To a maid engaged to Joseph, The angel Gabriel came.
"Fear not," the angel told her, "I come to bring good news.
Good news I come to tell you, Good news, I say, good news."
—*"To a Maid Engaged to Joseph," verse 1**

Then Mary said, "I am the Lord's servant. Let it be with me
just as you have said." Then the angel left her.
—*Luke 1:38*

First, a game of What If:

—Have you ever wondered, "What if the American Colonies had lost the Revolutionary War? Would we be breaking for tea and crumpets or paying with pounds?
—What if Rosa Parks never sat or Martin Luther King never marched?
—What if Jonas Salk did not cure polio or Alexander Fleming did not discover penicillin?
—What if Martin Luther hadn't nailed his ninety-five theses to the church door or John Wesley hadn't visited that chapel on Aldersgate Street that night?
—What if you were born to different parents? In another country?

What if, what if, what if?
And then there are others for us to ponder during this season of Advent:

—What if Joseph said, "Look, I wasn't born yesterday. I know how she had to have gotten pregnant. There's no way I'm getting involved with this."

—What if the shepherds said, "Um . . . we're just shepherds. We've got zero credibility in that town. No one would believe us, even if we did decide to go visit this 'king.' We'll pass."

—What if the magi said, "We don't need to follow some star. We'll find our own way."

And here's the biggest "What if?" of all: What if Mary said, "I'm sorry, there, Gabriel. You're going to have to find another girl. I've got too much of a future ahead of me to be bogged down by this."

Who knows if God would have gone to another young girl if Mary said no. But this is certain: Mary's single act of obedience was the lynchpin that set in motion a series of faithful actions by everyone else in the birth narrative. Jesus was, therefore, born into a family in which submission to God was in the DNA. Mary exhibited it, Joseph demonstrated it, and Jesus himself would eventually embody it on the cross.

When it came to learning obedience, Jesus was born into good earthly stock. And it all started with Mary.

That is the main subject of the Advent hymn "To a Maid Engaged to Joseph." Its six verses summarize the beautiful gospel encounter between Mary and the angel Gabriel known as the annunciation. In this first verse, we hear of the angel's first words to Mary: "Do not fear, for I bring you good news." What follows is the critical story in the birth narrative in which Mary says yes to God and agrees to bear the Word made flesh.

Orthodox traditions name her as the *Theotokos*, or "bearer of God." Christian doctrine is careful to specify that Mary's bearing of Jesus does not make her older than God, the creator of God, the source of Christ's divinity, or even divine herself. It simply means that she was the vessel through which God gave the world God's best, most complete self-revelation of love for humanity. Without Mary bearing the Word, the world would not know love in the Word made flesh.

Frederick Buechner, in his book *Peculiar Treasures*, wrote this about the angel's visit with Mary:

She struck the angel Gabriel as hardly old enough to have a child at all, let alone this child, but he'd been entrusted with a message to give her and he gave it. He told her what the child was to be named, and who he was to be, and something about the mystery that was to come upon her. "You mustn't be afraid, Mary," he said. And as he said it, he only hoped she wouldn't notice that beneath the great, golden wings, he himself was trembling with fear to think that the whole future of creation hung now on the answer of a girl.[1]

The answer of a girl.

Freedom of choice, the exercise of free will, has always been at the top of God's priority list when it comes to interaction with human beings. God would never force a yes from anyone and would never trick anyone into a response of love. That's the way God has been from the beginning.

God would even allow people to continue in their own disobedience, turn them over to their own ideas of how to make their own way, to get their own way, to find themselves in the prison of their own designs, to hit bottom if necessary, if only to give them a firm place from which to say, "Okay, yes. Your will be done."

And now all of this culminates in this moment, when an angel stands before a girl, answering her questions, as he and all the angelic host and even God wait. Will she do it? Will she say, yes?

We know the answer Mary gave: "I am the Lord's servant. Let it be with me just as you have said."

The reason we can herald Mary is not because she was divine, or that she created God, or that she was older than God. We can celebrate Mary because she said yes. When she had the freedom to say no, when the knowledge that all the people around her would surely look down on her and pressure her to say no, and when all her sensibilities were pushing her to say no, she said yes.

When we present ourselves as God's servants and are open to hearing what God asks of us, we will take our places in a long line of faithful people who have done just that. Then we will find ourselves set free to perform both small and large acts of care and compassion. We will be available for the adventures God has in store for us, for the work God needs us to do, and the work God has designed us, uniquely, to do.

That's the beauty of it. Even though you may never have thought about what God is asking of you, it doesn't mean that God hasn't been preparing you to do it. And don't think the angels aren't all holding their breath to hear your answer when God approaches you with a task. And don't think—just because you can't hear it—that all the heavenly hosts aren't singing, "Alleluia!" when you say, freely, yes.

Reflection

How can you begin to exhibit the kind of obedience Mary displayed? Have you ever thought of yourself as having the potential for "bearing" a word for God? How difficult is it for you to think of yourself with that kind of capability?

Prayer

Gracious and loving God, thank you for the example of Mary. Teach me to follow her example and to be obedient to you. Amen.

26

God's Ultimate Playlist

Read Luke 1:39–56

"For you are highly favored by God, the Lord of all,
who even now is with you. You are on earth most blest,
You are most blest, most blessed, God chose you, you are blest!"
— *"To a Maid Engaged to Joseph," verse 2**

Mary got up and hurried to a city in the Judean highlands. She
entered Zechariah's home and greeted Elizabeth. When Elizabeth heard Mary's greeting, the child leaped in her womb, and
Elizabeth was filled with the Holy Spirit.

—Luke 1:39–41

Sometimes, it might be possible to approach the Bible with too
much reverence.

That might seem odd for a preacher to say. After all, the
Bible is our primary doctrinal authority. It is the sacred source
for all that is necessary for our salvation and a foundation of
our faith.

Of course we are going to approach it reverently and soberly.

Except this: some passages want to be treated with more
than reverence. Sometimes, some stories are designed to be
subversive, surprising, imaginative, and even dangerous; and
these stories, therefore, expect us to react in the same way.

That is the case with this text from Luke 1, rendered in verse
2 of the hymn "To a Maid Engaged to Joseph." Luke 1 contains one of the most cherished, honored, and revered passages
of Scripture in the entire Bible.

Verses 46–55 of today's passage are widely referred to as
the Magnificat, which refers to the first few words of the song
of Mary: "My soul magnifies the Lord" (v. 46b NRSV). This
song follows the annunciation, in which the angel Gabriel

visits Mary and greets her with the words, "Rejoice, favored one!" (v. 28), famously rendered as, "Hail, Mary, full of grace."

Hail, Mary. Those words have been cherished and revered for countless generations: uttered innumerable times when praying the rosary, prescribed by priests as part of confessionals, and the only passage of Scripture to have a football play named after it.

But think about the context for this song by Mary. She is singing it, not as a solo, not to the angel, but to her relative Elizabeth. You know Elizabeth; she is married to a priest named Zechariah, and the two of them found out that they were pregnant. Except Elizabeth is old and barren and way past child-bearing years.

And Mary, though deemed a *virgin* in many of our translations, is more accurately characterized as a "young girl" in the original Hebrew text. She's probably thirteen or fourteen years old, way too young to be thinking about starting a family, at least in our modern ears.

So here is this magnificent scene in Luke 1:39, in which we have two pregnant women who really have no rational reason to be pregnant.

Mary was too young. Elizabeth was too old.

Mary wasn't even old enough to drive. Elizabeth probably shouldn't.

Mary just got her high school ID card. Elizabeth has her AARP card.

Mary has her whole life ahead of her. Elizabeth can't imagine a whole life inside her.

So you see, the way Luke tells it, this story isn't intended to be revered from a distance. No, this story is much too wonderfully wild and richly ridiculous and astonishingly absurd. It is meant to surprise us, unlock our imaginations, and push us to see the world and our lives in a completely new way.

That's why, when Mary walks into Elizabeth's room, there's no reverence, no genuflecting, no bowing, no slipping off of the shoes to stand on holy ground. Instead, when Mary walks in to Elizabeth's house all heaven breaks loose.

Elizabeth bursts out screaming. She explodes with emotion. And her baby turns her womb into a bouncy castle. "God has blessed you above all women, and he has blessed the child you carry" (v. 42).

Luke wants to make it perfectly clear: we aren't watching an episode of *60 Minutes*. We're watching a reunion episode of Oprah, because these two women don't know how to contain themselves.

And that is precisely what Luke wants from us for a moment. To shed all the stale veneers of pompous and proper behavior and allow ourselves to get even a little bit excited about what God wants to do in us and through us in this broken world.

Mary is so overcome by emotion and so blown away by a screaming Elizabeth and her somersaulting baby that all she can do is start singing. Her song is an echo of other songs we have heard from other biblical heroines throughout history.

There's Miriam, in the book of Exodus, the symbolic mother of the wandering Israelite slaves, who sings a song the very moment that the Israelites escape Pharaoh by crossing the Red Sea and stepping on to dry land.

There's Hannah, the mother of the great prophet Samuel, who would usher in the great kingdom of David. She has no business being pregnant either, but when she is pregnant with Samuel, she sings a song of great joy.

And now here's Mary, who first starts singing about how blessed she is but quickly changes to start singing about God.

What do all three of these songs have in common? They all sing about God's greatness. All of them sing about God's power and presence. They are all sung melodically and joyfully, and imaginatively and exuberantly, but here's the twist: They all put evil on alert and tell the world it better watch out, because God is going to do something great through ordinary people.

Miriam calls out Pharaoh in Exodus 15:1:

I will sing to the LORD, for an overflowing victory!
　　Horse and rider he threw into the sea!

Hannah puts the world on notice in 1 Samuel 2:9b–10a:

[T]he wicked die in darkness
　　because no one succeeds by strength alone.

The LORD!
His enemies are terrified!
　　God thunders against them from heaven!
The LORD!
He judges the far corners of the earth!

And here is Mary:

He has shown strength with his arm.
　　He has scattered those with arrogant thoughts and
　　　　proud inclinations.
　　He has pulled the powerful down from their thrones
　　　　and lifted up the lowly.
He has filled the hungry with good things
　　and sent the rich away empty-handed.

(Luke 1:51–53)

These songs are not to be venerated from a distance, like an idol from afar. These songs are calls to action meant to jolt us awake, shock us with their absurdity, and motivate us to stop sitting back and settling for the world as it is and to see the world in which God has already acted.

This song of Mary is no lullaby. It is a pep talk, a half-time speech, and God's way to tell you and me that we are Mary in this story, and we need to be servants of the Most High.

Reflection

How does seeing the uncanny, outlandish dimensions of this story help you experience the story of Mary and Elizabeth in a more powerful way? What other connections can you make among the songs of Miriam, Hannah, and Mary?

Prayer

Loving God, help me to sing a song of hope and defiance in the midst of suffering and evil. Teach me to see the ongoing work of your Spirit in this world and in my life. Amen.

27

The Call of Christmas

Read Luke 2:8–14

As Mary heard the angel, she wondered at his words.
"Behold, I am your handmaid," she said unto her God.
"So be it; I am ready according to your Word."
— *"To a Maid Engaged to Joseph," verse 6**

The angel said, "Don't be afraid! Look! I bring good news to
you—wonderful, joyous news for all people."
—Luke 2:10

We now find ourselves on this Advent journey just one day
away from Christmas Eve. Along the way, we have read and
experienced the poetry of some of the great hymns of the season. It seems appropriate, then, to conclude our tour of these
Advent songs with a different kind of poem. It is a rhyming
rendition of the Christmas story, to enliven the story of Mary
and Joseph captured in "To a Maid Engaged to Joseph." It
prompts this question: In what ways might you be called to be
like Mary and Joseph and be a bearer of the Word today?

In a time when the world was in chaos and fear
In a time when the people were all saddened with tears

In a time with no hope, when all yearned to be free
Does it sound like today? On this we would agree.

With no bells and no whistles, no tinsel, no gifts
Comes Jesus, for giving our spirits a lift.

And what is most special, and fills us with awe
Is the way that God chose to draw near to us all.

God came through some people, just like you and like me,
Not special-brand people, from good family trees.

You see, Mary and Joseph are some great Bible heroes,
But they're no more uncommon than us Mary's and Joe's.

When God's love became real in a most holy birth,
God chose plain, simple folks, the most common on earth.

So it shows that when God does extraordinary deeds
God prefers to use folks just like you and like me.

You don't need special training, or a call to the cloth;
You don't need to use words like "Thus sayeth" and "Doth";

You don't need to be rich or be saddled with wealth;
You don't need to be young with athletic good health;

You don't need to have mysteries all figured and clear;
You don't need strong experience or be seasoned with years.

All God wants from you now is a true, open heart
To say yes to the Lord when God gives you your part

In a tension-filled world that is battered and bruised,
In a time when deep anger and resentment are fused,

When we wonder how God might redeem us again,
When we wonder how God might save us from sin.

If we wonder how Jesus will come make the way straight
Or which Mary and Joseph will rise up today.

There is only one answer, from the Bible we've heard
That we're Joseph and Mary, and we bear God's Word.

Will you choose today to say yes to God's call?
To say yes to the one who was born in a stall?

Will you not wait to have it all start to make sense,
And, like Mary, declare to God obedience?

Will you ignore all the risk and what others might say,
And, with Joseph-like faith, say you'll do it God's way?

The world needs Christ today, of that there's no doubt.
The Christ that's within you, you must boldly give out.

If all this world wants for this Christmas is hope,
And if all that it wants is a way to all cope,

Then let's share with them news of a faithful new friend,
This Jesus, Messiah, the most special Godsend.

In the name of our God who created the heavens,
And redeems us, sustains us, we all say, Amen.

Reflection

With what excuses do you try to convince yourself that you are
not worthy of God's call on your life? What actions will you
take to overcome those excuses and say yes to God today?

Prayer

*God, once again you come into the world in the most unsuspected
way. I welcome you into my heart. Amen.*

28

Christmas Eve
A Most Unusual Gift

Read Luke 2:15–20

Silent night, holy night! All is calm, all is bright
'round yon virgin mother and child!
Holy Infant, so tender and mild,
sleep in heavenly peace, sleep in heavenly peace.
— *"Silent Night," verse 1*

They went quickly and found Mary and Joseph, and
the baby lying in the manger. When they saw this, they
reported what they had been told about this child. Everyone
who heard it was amazed at what the shepherds told them.
— *Luke 2:16–18*

We have finally made it to Christmas Eve. After all the craziness and chaos and all of the flurry of activity, it is finally, officially, appropriate to wish everyone a Merry Christmas and sing those Christmas carols, starting with the mainstay of all traditional Christmas Eve services: "Silent Night."

If I were with you in person, I would want to present to you a special Christmas gift. You can thank me later. Do you want to know what it is?

It's a fruitcake! Aren't you excited? No? Okay.

I suppose there is no more controversial, if not vilified, holiday food product than this one. For folks who would rather gnaw on a brick with a bow on it than dig into a fruitcake, maybe it's time to give this Christmas concoction its due. And maybe learn an important lesson to conclude our Advent reflections.

Food historians trace the first example of the fruitcake to ancient Egypt, when compacted, dense cakes of nuts and berries were buried with the sarcophagi of deceased nobility. I imagine that archaeologists discovered evidence of this on the wall of a mummy's tomb, where hieroglyphics revealed the following proverb: Fruitcake? You've gotta be dead to want this!

Flash forward to ancient Rome, where the fruitcake was a product of the fall harvest; cakes were made to sustain soldiers through the long winter. I suspect that throughout the entire period of the Roman Empire, only one fruitcake was actually created and then re-gifted throughout the legions of soldiers.

Today, there are lots of recipes for making fruitcakes and lots of ingredients that can go into them: candied cherries, sliced almonds, raisins, chocolate chips, molasses, apricots, shoe leather, sawdust, and fish guts. . . . I'm just kidding . . . about the molasses.

But here's the one thing that many of the recipes have in common: At the end of the cooking time, you invert the cake pan. The cake is let out to cool, as its bottom becomes the top. The top becomes the bottom. The whole cake is turned upside down.

Come to think of it, the fruitcake may not be such a bad symbol for Christmas after all.

It was about two thousand years ago, when the people of God longed for a deliverer—a person who would come and break them free from their oppression and crush their oppressors. Instead, they received a deliverer who took their expectations and flipped them on their ears, reversing their definition of *redeemer*.

They were expecting a king to come on horseback, with the fanfare of trumpets and the strength of a thousand armies. Instead, they got a king born in the back alley in a feeding trough, amid the stench of sheep and cows, with the frailty and innocence of a newborn child.

On this silent night long ago, the word of God became flesh, dwelt among us, and took every expectation, every preconceived notion that we had, and inverted it. Jesus came to turn things upside down, bringing a vision of calm and bright amid the chaos and noise of our broken world.

He would grow up not to follow his father's work as a

carpenter but to become a rabbi, a preacher, a miracle healer, and our Messiah.

He would constantly preach the inversion of human reality and the conversion of human souls:

> "So those who are last will be first. And those who are first will be last." (Matt. 20:16)

> "Those who find their lives will lose them, and those who lose their lives because of me will find them." (Matt. 10:39)

> "If people slap you on your right cheek, you must turn the left cheek to them as well." (Matt. 5:39)

> "[T]he Human One didn't come to be served but rather to serve and to give his life to liberate many people." (Matt. 20:28)

The birth of this child two thousand years ago turned the world upside down, and he has continued doing it ever since through his life, death, and resurrection. In fact, he is still doing it today.

There are people dying daily from poverty and hunger, people bullied and rejected for being different, people grieving the loss of a loved one, a job, a home. There are people in the world living under the constant threat of violence, fearful that it will erupt any moment, in the streets, from the sky, and within their homes. But there is good news: Violence will give way to heavenly peace, and calm will subvert chaos.

Do you begin to see the power, the impact, and the drama this one moment in history continues to have throughout time? This Jesus has never stopped lifting up the lowly and toppling the proud; raising up the downtrodden and bringing down the powerful; even taking the rough, disheveled, and messy parts of your own life and putting them back together.

What does Christ need to invert within your life today? Perhaps you continue to grieve the loss of a loved one, deal with the pain of a fractured relationship, battle an ongoing addiction, or try to sweep away a haunting memory that will not fade.

Jesus comes to turn your world upside down, to break in a word of hope against all your despair, to calm your anxiety, and to overwhelm you with a light that will pierce even your greatest darkness—in short, to give you peace.

Reflection

What does Jesus want to "turn upside down" in your life? Where can you spread the light of Christ's hope and peace in a despairing world?

Prayer

Dear God, thank you for coming into our world as a tiny baby and reigning in our lives. I receive you with joy; now help me share you with others. Amen.

Notes

Chapter 1: Forgive and Forget?
1. Anne Frank, *The Diary of a Young Girl* (New York: Knopf Publishing Group, 1995), 56.

Chapter 5: Prepare the Way
1. Rob Bell, "Noise," Nooma 5, http://nooma.com/films/005-noise.

Chapter 6: Desensitized to Hope
1. C. S. Lewis, *The Last Battle* (New York: HarperCollins, 2002), 181.
2. Ibid., 185.

Chapter 9: Jesus' Inaugural Address
1. Wang Chien-Chuang, "The Right Words at the Right Time," *Taipei Times*, April 26, 2000, http://www.taipeitimes.com/News /editorials/archives/2000/04/26/0000033725/1.

Chapter 10: Why Worry?
1. St. Francis de Sales, *Wise and Loving Counsels* (Mahwah, NJ: Paulist Press, 1971), 16.

Chapter 12: Claiming the Future
1. Margaret Sangster, *Good Manners for All Occasions: A Practical Manual* (Cornell University Press, 2009), 177.

Chapter 15: The Return of the King
1. "Prophecy: What the Bible Says about the End of the World," *Newsweek*, October 25, 1999.

Chapter 16: What? Me, Holy?
1. John Brown, *Expository Discourses on the First Epistle of the Apostle Peter* (New York: Robert Carter & Brothers, 1855), 117.

2. John Wesley, "On the Wedding Garment," in *John Wesley's Sermons* (Nashville: Abingdon Press, 2010), 559.

Chapter 18: Choose or Refuse

1. Freeborn Garrettson, "A Short Account of My Life till I Was Justified by Faith" in Lester Ruth, *Early Methodist Life and Spirituality: A Reader"* (Nashville: Kingswood Books, 2005), 205–11.

Chapter 19: Hopefully

1. Geoff Nunberg, "The Word 'Hopefully' Is Here to Stay," *NPR*, May 30, 2012, http://www.npr.org/2012/05/30/153709651/the-word-hopefully-is-here-to-stay-hopefully.

Chapter 20: Called to Do Better

1. Denise Chow, "Astronaut Husband of Rep. Gabrielle Giffords, "There's Little That We Can Do but Pray," SPACE.com, January 10, 2011, http://www.space.com/10589-astronaut-husband-rep-gabrielle-giffords-pray.html.

2. *The United Methodist Hymnal* (Nashville: The United Methodist Publishing House, 1989), 34.

Chapter 23: God's Answer to Suffering

1. Walter Isaacson, *Steve Jobs* (New York: Simon & Shuster, 2011), 14.

Chapter 24: Personal, Not Digital

1. Gary Small and Gigi Vorgan, "Your iBrain: How Technology Changes the Way We Think," *Scientific American Mind*, October 1, 20008, http://www.scientificamerican.com/article/your-ibrain/.

2. Ibid.

Chapter 25: She Said Yes

1. Frederick Buechner, *Peculiar Treasures* (New York: HarperOne, 1993), 49.

CPSIA information can be obtained
at www.ICGtesting.com
Printed in the USA
BVHW031114051220
594962BV00004B/54

9 780664 262525